POLITICS
AND
ECONOMICS
In an
INTERDEPENDENT WORLD

Arthur Ross

POLITICS
AND
ECONOMICS
In an
INTERDEPENDENT WORLD

Collected Papers
of
ARTHUR ROSS

Preface by
Senator Jacob K. Javits

Introduction by
Sir Fitzroy Maclean

Distributed by the University of Pennsylvania Press
Published in 1978
©
Copyright, 1978
by
Arthur Ross

Library of Congress Catalog Card Number: 78-24281
ISBN: 0-8122-7762-7

CONTENTS

AUTHOR'S NOTE

The papers in this volume were presented during the past fourteen years on the occasion of various public and business activities. They are reprinted here with changes only for the sake of clarity or contemporary reference. Thus some are "period pieces," which, I believe, have some relevance today. A final essay entitled "The U.S. Sino-Soviet Triangle: A Vision for the Future" has been written for this volume.

To Al, Bev, and Cliff

BIOGRAPHICAL NOTES

ARTHUR ROSS, an investment banker, is vice chairman of the Gottesman-Central National Organization and managing director of the Central National Corporation, a group of international companies with a substantial investment portfolio specializing in the world-wide marketing of pulp and paper. Mr. Ross was born in New York in 1910, attended the Wharton School of Business at the University of Pennsylvania, and received the bachelor of science degree from Columbia University (1931). During World War II, he served as a lieutenant commander in the U.S. Navy from 1942-45. A frequent member of the United States delegation to the United Nations Economic and Social Council, Mr. Ross was senior adviser to the United States delegation at UNESCO's Eighteenth Biennial Conference in Paris (1974). He currently serves as a consultant on economic and social affairs to the United States Mission to the United Nations and has testified as an expert witness before Congressional committees on economic growth and international trade. In addition to his business and international affairs interests, Mr. Ross has taken an active philanthropic role in medical care, museums, educational institutions, parks and horticultural development; he is a member of a number of corporate as well as civic boards of directors. Mr. Ross, who is the father of Alfred F., Beverly, and Clifford Arthur, lives in New York City and East Hampton, New York.

JACOB K. JAVITS is the senior United States senator from the state of New York. He was born in New York City in 1904, graduated from New York University Law School (1926), practiced law in New York City, and served in the U.S. Army as a major and then as a lieutenant colonel in the United States and in the European and Pacific theatres during World War II. In 1946 he was elected to the 30th Congress of the United States from the Twenty-first New York congressional district. He served in the House of Representatives for four terms before being elected attorney general of the state of New York in 1954. Two years later he was elected to the United States Senate where he is now serving his fourth six-year term. He is currently a member of the Senate Foreign Relations, Governmental Affairs, Human Resources and Joint Economic committees. Among many other activities, Senator Javits has been a United States delegate to the United Nations General Assembly and chairman of the North Atlantic Assembly's "Committee of Nine," which evaluated the future of NATO.

SIR FITZROY MACLEAN was born in 1911 and educated at Eton and Cambridge. He entered the British diplomatic service in 1933, serving at the Foreign Office and in Paris and Moscow. After the outbreak of war, he enlisted as a private in the Cameron Highlanders and rising to the rank of brigadier, was twice parachuted into German-occupied Yugoslavia where he was Winston Churchill's personal representative and commanded the British Military Mission to Tito's partisans. From 1941 to 1974 he was a Conservative member of parliament, serving as Under-Secretary of State for War in the Churchill and Eden governments. From 1964 to 1974 he was chairman of the Military Committee of the North Atlantic Assembly. His books include *Eastern Approaches, A Concise History of Scotland, Take Nine Spies* and *Holy Russia.* Sir Fitzroy has received a number of decorations from his own and foreign governments and was created a baronet in 1957. He resides in Argyll, Scotland.

PREFACE
JACOB K. JAVITS

I have been interested always in the boldness and unconventionality with which Arthur Ross, by training and inclination a conventional investment banker, has approached economic facts at home and abroad. I am pleased that his thinking, until now available only to a small circle of colleagues, is being presented here to a wider audience.

Essentially, Arthur Ross' deep conviction is that through the business system the world can be redeemed from what is still, for most, endemic poverty.

He has no hangups about governmental controls, or fears of so-called "socialism," either of which might intimidate a lesser man. For example, even when referring to his own fundamentally conservative training and values, he still finds that public authorities have been unable adequately to monitor or control the global range of corporate operations. He presents a searching analysis of the way the multinational corporate network—so much of it based in the United States— is capable of vaulting over national borders. He shows convincingly how the mission of moving capital and technology in response to economic needs can be the greatest contributor to the efficient operation of the global economic system. What is even more important, he shows that it is the multinational corporations, rather than governments, that have established a record of achievement for supplying the wants of peoples everywhere.

Fundamental to his thinking, and what gives it its unique flavor, is his deep feeling that the profit motive alone, without adequate social controls, will not achieve the social objectives of society—and this view is held at the same time that he is thoroughly committed

1

to a market economy. He recognizes that, unchecked by social considerations, real economic progress, in human terms, is limited. But when social considerations are included there is much greater stability, permanence, satisfaction, and finally, achievement.

Arthur Ross does not extend his essays to the methods by which these social controls shall be effected. But he gives us every clear indication of a deeply imbedded confidence in democratic systems, which when coupled with adequate information and education will accomplish that purpose. He constantly exhibits a perceptive analysis of international issues and a rare sensitivity to coming trends.

During our long friendship, I have become impressed as well with Arthur Ross' specific knowledge of Moslem and Arab cultures and histories, and with his respect for their influence on the future performance of the Islamic countries. They now influence so much of our destiny through their control of the world's oil resources.

I have constantly benefited by Arthur Ross' perceptiveness. He was among the first in the business and financial community to recognize the growing interdependence among the industrialized nations of Western Europe, the United States, and Japan. He foresaw their growing interdependence with the developing countries and the complexities of that relationship, which has become one of the great problems of the present world economic situation.

I am fascinated too by Arthur Ross' lack of bias. He presents, for example, in the essay on "Dueling and Dealing with the Russians," a completely objective picture of the advantages of assisting in the economic development of the Soviet Union and its Eastern European allies, as well as of Mainland China. He urges us to understand that if we believe in interdependence, we must include also, as a matter of our own self-interest, interdependence with the vast Sino-Soviet bloc of more than one and a half billion people.

His insight, character, and objectivity in dealing with

political and economic issues, constantly in evidence in these essays, have made Arthur Ross a valued advisor to the United States Mission to the United Nations and to the various U.S. delegations to U.N. conferences on which he has served as a public member. His is an international outlook which remains optimistic because of his belief in the capability of the market system under intelligent social controls to bring about a higher state of economic well being for all peoples on the basis of mutuality and self-interest, the very hallmarks of modern international economics.

Arthur Ross shows himself in these pages to be truly what we called in earlier days a "merchant prince," that is, a statesman who has turned to business and finance as the outlet for his creativity and his talents. He cannot accept the fact that two billion of the world's four billion people are seemingly sentenced to poverty. He proposes the means by which this sentence may be remitted and they may be redeemed. It is universalist and practical, building upon the strongest of our existing foundations—the economic system of the free world. It is also a philosophic concept which rejects the exclusion of the communist world, but proposes the terms upon which it may be incorporated into a worldwide economic community of man.

We often have been referred to in the United States as a nation whose business is business. Arthur Ross brings to this description a nobility of concept. It could be described as recognizing the character of the United States and its people, and putting that quality to work in new ways to make it a major, affirmative value for the whole world.

Finally, Arthur Ross is an evangel of peace with a practical evaluation of how peace may be brought about. He makes it clear that the principal threat to peace is the competition between the communist and capitalist systems as epitomized by the three superpowers, the Soviet Union, the United States, and China.

He perceives that even superior to the evangelism of

communism is the appeal to the peoples in the European communist bloc and China of a higher state of well being. He believes that this can be attained, without compromising their system or ours, through economic relations built upon an intelligent platform that requires peace to make the relationship tenable and credit-worthy. This is a key point with Arthur Ross. He therefore comes to a logical conclusion. For, in essence he is a logician. He thinks that if we are to utilize western capital and finance to enable the Soviet Union to develop its economic potential and its resources, then they must agree to a sharp and dramatic reduction in all kinds of armaments as a part of a new framework of cooperation in economic areas. He brings China's emergent economic and security needs into this complex equation in an equivalent pragmatic fashion.

As a friend, business and financial leader, statesman, and philosopher, Arthur Ross has earned our gratitude and appreciation and has made a profound contribution in mapping the economic road ahead. He has shown us, I think convincingly, the right road—the road of interdependence, credit-worthiness, reciprocity, peace, and the capacity of man to arrange for his own redemption from poverty and war.

Arthur Ross has the aura of a high-level executive and he is, in fact, managing director and vice chairman of Central National Corporation, where his colleagues have encouraged these far-ranging inquiries. But beyond his corporate and business interests his plans for economic action are those of a renaissance man, an artist in his own field. I believe that the reader will find this broad perspective pervading all of the essays contained in this collection.

Washington, D.C.   J. K. J.
July 1978

INTRODUCTION

SIR FITZROY MACLEAN

The nineteenth century saw the rise of national feeling and the nation state. World War I convinced the nations, or rather some of them, of the need for a greater measure of international cooperation. The result was the League of Nations, which over the next twenty years effectively proved its inability to perform the task for which it had been created, namely, to keep the peace and deter aggression. World War II, which put the League of Nations out of business, also helped it to rise from its own ashes in the shape of the United Nations, which, like its predecessor, has for the last thirty years and more met with only limited success in most of its more important undertakings. Ironically enough, a far greater influence for peace has been the balance of terror imposed on East and West alike by their mutual possession of the nuclear deterrent.

Little wonder, then, that over the years most people have lost confidence in international organizations in a peace-keeping role. Nor is this all. To a lot of people internationalism in almost any field has long been suspect. To right wingers it suggests that the now nominally defunct Comintern or Communist International, which in their eyes typified the international revolutionary conspiracy they feared, would one day overthrow all they held most dear. Nor has the proudly proclaimed internationalism of most present-day terrorists done anything to reassure them.

For their counterparts on the left the bogey is of course international finance: the great cartels which know no frontiers or loyalties except to mammon; the food producers who, it is said, burn food to keep its price up, rather than let it be eaten by starving millions; and the arms dealers, the merchants of death, who sell their

5

products indiscriminately to both sides. In short, it is not too much to say that over the years internationalism has become something very like a dirty word. Nor is it of much avail in this context to point to the limited but still very real success in breaking down political frontiers achieved by the members of the European Economic Community. That, too, has its detractors.

How refreshing, therefore, to find in Arthur Ross someone who has the courage to speak up for financial and economic internationalism, for more trade and aid between the nations, regardless of ideology and political differences, and for joint international economic, financial, and other action in a whole range of different fields, and who does so with such an obvious grasp of his subject.

The theme of Arthur Ross' book is interdependence, the interdependence which, whether we like it or not, is already a fact and which, if accepted and exploited rather than resisted, can bring great benefits to humanity. And here his argument is soundly based, for the simple reason that international cooperation based on solid mutual economic benefit is far more likely to succeed than the theoretical internationalism of the U.N. and the League of Nations. What is more, it is also more likely to bring in the long run the international political stability we aim at.

The author opens with a reasoned defense of the multinational corporations, which ten years or more ago already provided the principal channel by which capital from one country could be invested in another, thereby furnishing the most convenient means of promoting economic development internationally. Inevitably the lack of alternative sources of capital led to a dependence on the multinationals which came to be resented by countries in search of development funds and gave rise to a good deal of criticism of the multinationals, some of it justified. In the first of three papers written in 1971, 1973, and 1975 respectively, Mr.

Ross meets this criticism and suggests specific remedies where remedies are required, his contention being that, if properly regulated, the multinational corporation offers the best, if not the only, means of encouraging development internationally. International companies, he points out, with a growth rate in excess of national growth rates, had ten years ago already internationalized an important sector of world production, the process being accelerated by the situation prevailing in Europe and elsewhere at the end of World War II and also by the immense improvements in international communications of all kinds. As he himself puts it, "We are committed to a system, not only of international trade, but also of international production."

This was a fact of life which could not be altered. Moreover, provided that proper regard was had for social and other human considerations and that the profit motive was not allowed to override all other objectives, the multinationals could, by increasing production, not only bring greater prosperity and a better standard of living to the various countries concerned, but could also help to unify and reconcile the aims and aspirations of their peoples at least as effectively as their respective governments were doing. Nor, for that matter, should the profit motive be thoughtlessly condemned. As Mr. Ross most pertinently points out, "more has been accomplished for the benefit of mankind by the engine of the profit motive than by appealing to the humanitarian feelings of either the East or the West."

There were, of course, dangers and difficulties involved, as in any human course of action. One danger, or so it was claimed, was that in the developing countries the intervention of the multinationals would lead to the ruthless exploitation of their human and material resources by greedy outsiders, to the wholesale disregard of ecological and other social considerations and to the establishment in certain important sectors of world production of virtual monopolies calculated to deter effective competition. But these, once again, are difficulties that can be overcome, always provided that the necessary rules are made and observed.

Addressing himself to the NATO countries in the first of his articles on this subject, written in 1971, and in particular to the governments of the United States and Western Europe, between them responsible for approximately two-thirds of total world output, the author goes on to urge that the scope of the multinational corporate network should be extended to include the less developed countries, the Soviet bloc, and China, together accounting for the remaining thirty-odd percent.

This is obviously easier said than done. The developing nations are, for their part, inclined to be suspicious of foreign aid, believing that what the West is after is their raw materials and that, instead of carrying out intermediate and final manufacturing processes in their countries, the multinationals would use them mainly as a source of raw material, thus discouraging their industrial development and condemning them to perpetual poverty. They are also inclined to doubt the efficacy in this context of capitalism or free enterprise, distrusting the unfettered operation of market forces and preferring to seek a solution to their problems in some carefully planned socialist Utopia. Nor are the hesitations all on one side. Not unnaturally, the multinationals are inclined to think twice before committing themselves too deeply to countries of dubious political stability.

But Mr. Ross, who is by nature an optimist, is convinced that, with enough good will on both sides, these difficulties can be overcome, just as he believes that it should be possible to overcome the political and ideological obstacles that stand in the way of a greater degree of economic integration between the West and the Soviet bloc. "Economics," he writes, " is the interplay of competing opportunities for the use of resources. Those opportunities are no less real as they occur in Western, Eastern, or Third World areas." "Politics," he concludes hopefully, "may complicate economics, but can rarely nullify it."

Another subject on which Mr. Ross has some very pertinent things to say is ecology. Like economics, this is an aspect of world affairs which should logically transcend political and ideological barriers. And here I am glad to be able to report from my own recent experience that, in discussing ecological problems with Soviet delegations, my colleagues and I have found that our Soviet interlocutors were prepared in the end to abandon their original contention that industrial pollution only occurred under capitalism—an argument which it was manifestly hard for them to sustain in full view of Soviet industrial plants belching out, as we watched, heavy clouds of greasy black smoke. But pollution is far from being the only problem. We cannot afford to forget that the basic materials of this planet are finite. Once again the problem affects us all and calls, as the author reminds us, for world analysis.

In any case, whether we like it or not, power is being increasingly concentrated in multinational corporations. Even if we wanted to, we could not simply go back to the old patterns of domestic production or investment. In this context the terms "foreign" and "domestic" are becoming ever more meaningless. Moreover, economic power cannot be divorced from political power. Though national governments sometimes have difficulty in grasping this, we are entering an era of international interdependence. Inevitably, different parts of the world are linked by vast movements of goods and services. Which means, in effect, that national governments will have a smaller part to play in the future than they have hitherto. On the other hand, it must not be forgotten that the multinationals have ceased to be monolithic. Instead, they operate as part of a corporate whole, and corporate decision-making is itself becoming more often than not an internationalized process.

But, though the present concentration of economic power has in a relatively short space of time produced vast material wealth, and though the multinational corporations have undoubtedly brought great benefits to humanity, we still have to find fairer ways of distributing the wealth they produce. In this respect, too, progress is being made. In May 1974, a special session of the United Nations General Assembly adopted a Declaration on the Establishment of a New Economic Order and promulgated a "Charter of Economic Rights and Duties of States." This was a first attempt to formulate a set of international rules to govern relations between national states and multinational corporations. It was followed shortly after by a full-scale debate in the Economic and Social Council of the United Nations on the impact of multinational corporations on development and on international relations, and it is not too much to say that this focused attention on the problem and provided, as it were, a blueprint for the developing world.

The subject of foreign aid is at least as controversial as that of multinational corporations. The author tackles it with the same forthrightness and optimism in three papers presented to the Economic and Political Committees of the NATO Parliamentarians or North Atlantic Assembly in the mid-nineteen-sixties. At that time the United States was contributing considerably more than half of all foreign aid to the developing world, while no other country's contribution amounted to more than eight percent. Recalling that foreign aid was regarded as a Cold War weapon and was administered in such a way as to encourage free enterprise in the recipient countries, Mr. Ross deplores this essentially ideological motive, which he describes as short-sighted, and expresses relief that it no longer prevails. Here I cannot help feeling that he is possibly under a misapprehension as to the true nature of what, over the past thirty years, has variously been described as Cold War, coexistence, and détente. Though the Americans come closer than most to such thoughtless benevolence, it is scarcely to be expected that any great power, however openhanded, would think of distributing foreign aid without a clearly defined political motive or without at any rate giving some thought to the probable consequences of its action.

Since soon after the end of World War II, a continuing ideological (and on occasion military) confrontation has been in progress between East and West. Sometimes this has been more and sometimes less acute. Indeed there have been periods when the Western powers have, rightly or wrongly, felt able to leave it largely out of account. But for the Russians it has continued to be a reality and it has for this reason never ceased to color every aspect of Soviet policy. Thus Soviet aid, when given, is invariably given from purely ideological motives and it is therefore only to be expected that corresponding considerations should influence Western policy decisions in the same field. Political strings attached to foreign aid are, it is true, apt to be counter-productive, but that they should be used by the West, where possible, to encourage free enterprise and democratic government seems to me only reasonable.

With this reservation, I find myself in agreement with the author's general conclusions. Aid, as he points out, should have a social connotation, should be linked to human development, should help to develop the potentialities of the countries that receive it, should, long-term, help to promote self-sufficiency. Care should also be taken that it really reaches the people of a country and does not, as so often in the past, remain in the hands of its rulers to be used by them to further their own private ends and purposes. With this in mind, the underdeveloped countries should be encouraged to cultivate their human resources. More and better education is a vital necessity, always provided that it is the right kind of education and calculated to produce the right results. In administering aid, sufficient flexibility must clearly be shown to meet a wide variety of different circumstances and situations.

The matter was already one of great urgency when

Mr. Ross began writing his articles fifteen years ago. Since then some progress has been made, it is true, but the problem nevertheless remains one of great urgency today. Despite the rapid advance of science and technology, despite the progress we have made in a dozen different fields, there are more people living in poverty today than there were fifty years ago, and by the end of the century the population of the underdeveloped countries will constitute an even higher percentage of the world's population than it does today.

The author concludes his section on foreign aid with a most necessary warning that the West and NATO, with their dwindling populations, should not neglect their own weaker brethren. Charity begins at home. The alliance is only as strong as its weakest link. To take only one example, a country in the condition in which Italy at present finds herself comes close to being a liability rather than an asset. And, here again, time is not on our side.

Today no study of the international political and economic situation could be complete without some reference to oil, to the energy crisis, and to the latest developments in the Middle East. But ten years ago, when Mr. Ross wrote the first of his papers on this subject, most Western politicians showed relatively little concern for it. In this paper, which is aptly entitled "NATO's Second Front" and which, as I well remember, he presented to a joint meeting of the Political and Military Committees of the North Atlantic Assembly in Paris in October 1968, he pointed out that, while in Western Europe NATO's defenses were relatively strong, in the Middle East, its response to Soviet penetration had been completely inadequate. He went on to stress the immense importance to the Alliance of ensuring the stability and tranquility of the region and so safeguarding trade routes and future oil supplies. For the Western powers, he wrote, the best way to limit Soviet influence was to play a more active part themselves. In this he showed considerable foresight. Indeed, had more attention been paid to some of the suggestions advanced in his paper, many of our later troubles might have been avoided.

Russia, as Mr. Ross says, has long had territorial and other ambitions in the Middle East. By 1968, she had already greatly strengthened her position in the whole area and was in particular beginning to build up her naval strength there in a way which Mr. Ross rightly found alarming. "If the Russian Mediterranean naval build-up continues," he wrote, "NATO's sea power in the region will be seriously challenged." He has since been proved abundantly right. As Admiral Gorshkov, the Soviet naval commander-in-chief put it recently, "Soviet sea power has become the optimum means to defeat the Imperialist enemy and the most important element in the Soviet arsenal to prepare the way for a Communist world...." Nothing, surely, could be clearer than that.

Looking back ten years later, with the benefit of accumulated hindsight, one cannot but endorse the conclusion Mr. Ross reached at the time, namely that even then the West was failing to meet the Soviet challenge with sufficient thrust or imagination; that NATO's reaction had been slow and sluggish; and that what was needed was a common NATO policy combining flexible approaches on the economic, diplomatic, and military fronts.

Equally to the point is the author's next paper, "Moslem Oil and the Yankee Dollar," which he presented to the North Atlantic Assembly at our Ankara meeting in September 1973. This was written immediately before the Arab oil embargo and the international crisis which followed it. In it, after quoting several sets of figures to illustrate the world's growing dependence on Arab and Middle Eastern oil and dwelling on the consequent enormous growth in the economic power of the oil-producing countries of the Middle East, he goes on to discuss the various problems arising from this situation and suggests ways in which the Western powers might meet them. Geographically, as he most pertinently points out, a high proportion of all Middle Eastern oil traffic is channeled through two narrow straits, both easily blockaded: the Strait of Hormuz which connects the Persian Gulf with the Gulf of Oman, and the Strait of Bab-el-Mandeb at the southern end of the Red Sea. This fact of geography clearly makes the situation even more precarious than it would otherwise be and places a high premium on the political stability of what, since Great Britain's departure, has become a notoriously unstable area, rendered even more unstable than it would otherwise have been by the Arab-Israeli conflict.

Quite apart from the manifest danger of Western oil supplies being cut off by political or military action, it was already obvious when Mr. Ross presented his paper to the North Atlantic Assembly that, so long as there were no other competitive sources of energy, the world price of oil would continue to rise and the accumulated wealth of the oil-producing countries would increase in proportion. Some of this wealth, as he pointed out, was by then already beginning to be invested abroad, notably in the United States and Western Europe.

Bearing in mind the long-term probability of declining world oil reserves, Mr. Ross sensibly suggests that as a first step the United States, Western Europe, and Japan should agree on a common oil policy providing for the creation of an oil consumers' union to negotiate with the oil producers, the restriction of oil consumption, and the joint development of all alternative sources of energy.

By February 1974, when the author next addressed himself to the subject, the energy crisis of the winter of 1973, which followed the Arab oil embargo, had already taken place. By this time an Arab-Israeli settlement seemed within reach, and it had become obvious that, so far as oil was concerned, the real problem would not be supply but high cost. The higher cost of this commodity, by its very nature, was bound to be passed on to a wide range of other commodities and so lead to gallop-

14

ing inflation with all its corrosive and generally dele-
terious side-effects, including a persistent balance of
payments crisis, which, as the author sadly remarks in a
postscript written four years later, "has engulfed us."

Returning to the theme of financial and economic
interdependence in a closely written paper presented in
1973, the author goes on to advocate more foreign
investment in the United States and, carrying his argument a stage further, more international and multinational investment worldwide. More direct foreign
investment in United States production facilities
would, he points out, not only alleviate the prevailing
shortage of capital and so help to increase production, it
would also go a long way toward solving the balance of
payments problem and induce greater monetary stability. (It would also, incidentally, provide an answer to
Jean-Jacques Servan-Schreiber's complaints of excessive American economic and financial influence in
Europe.) In general, more international investment
would, in a variety of ways, including what he terms
constructive competition, encourage technological
exchanges and promote international understanding.

International investment should, Mr. Ross suggests,
be encouraged by all governments by all available
means. Whether for this reason or by the simple operation of market forces, it is satisfying to note that there
has of late been a marked increase in direct foreign
investment in the United States, with corresponding
advantages for all concerned. Even so, the United States
continued to suffer from a shortage of capital, and, in a
statement before the Sub-Committee on Economic
Growth of the Economic Committee of Congress made
in May 1974, Mr. Ross reverted to this subject, advocat-
ing a number of measures which were required if the
country's capital base was to be sufficiently increased
and production correspondingly expanded. In this
statement, he also sturdily defends corporate profits as
essential for the provision of the capital necessary for
further development. "There is," he writes, with feeling

and with good sense, "a strong tendency to think that profits are something a business does not really need, or at least something that can be reduced without serious consequences"; and he goes on to explain the vital importance of such earnings for reinvestment and continuing development. Pointing out that American investment in productive facilities is, surprisingly, the lowest of the major industrial countries, and that the United States, again surprisingly, has the highest percentage of obsolete production facilities of any leading industrial nation, he urges on the United States government a series of fiscal measures, comparable to those already existing in a number of other countries and designed to encourage corporate investment and afford investors some protection against inflation. But, like other governments, the government of the United States is hard to convince that its wisest course lies in renouncing an assured source of revenue in the hope of eventual long-term benefits; so far there have been regrettably few signs that Mr. Ross' cogent arguments have received the attention they deserve.

Mr. Ross completes his *tour d'horizon* of the international scene with three studies of East-West relations written in 1966, 1970, and 1977 respectively. His initial approach to this subject is characteristically optimistic. Thus in 1966, at a time when the Soviet Union had already embarked on the vast naval build-up already referred to, he felt able to advocate a step in the direction of unilateral disarmament on the part of NATO on the grounds that this would further the cause of détente and that the funds thus released could be more usefully used for social and economic purposes.

With this proposition I find myself (and found myself at the time) unable to agree. Disarmament is certainly desirable. But it must be mutual and balanced. For the NATO powers to weaken themselves unilaterally (and they are already—and were in 1966—far weaker than they should be) would be simply to invite Soviet aggression. On the other hand, I find it much easier to accept

16

the contention advanced in a paper submitted by Mr. Ross four years later to the Political and Economic Committees of the North Atlantic Assembly in which he suggests that the most promising opportunity for easing the strains between the NATO countries and their East European counterparts lies in increasing trade between them. "Trade," he writes, "intertwines the self-interests of both sides and promotes interdependence, an important bulwark of stability." With this I am inclined to agree, subject always to the proviso that the political and defense interests of the Western trade partner are adequately safeguarded in what could otherwise easily be an uneven bargain.

What is certainly true is that increased contacts between East and West, whether economic or cultural or simply human, tend to break down the ideological and political barriers between them and, one hopes, encourage the gradual evolution and, in the long run, liberalization of the Soviet and other Eastern bloc regimes. Furthermore, in the case of the satellites, for example, Rumania, trade with the West can offer a means of easing the economic bonds which tie them to the Soviet Union.

In his 1970 paper, Mr. Ross envisaged the extension of credit facilities as a means of increasing trade with the Eastern bloc. During the next seven years this took place on a considerable scale, with the result that by 1977 the Warsaw Pact countries owed the West some 45 billion dollars. No doubt he had not envisaged an extension of credit on such a scale, without military and political safeguards, and in his third article, published in the winter of that year, Mr. Ross examines the political and other implications of the resulting situation and finds them, not surprisingly, somewhat disquieting. Forty-three percent of Soviet purchases in the West, he tells us, consist of advanced technological products which enable the Soviet government to upgrade its industrial plant and increase the scale and sophistication of its armaments. Meanwhile, every year between

1970 and 1977 the Russians were spending more than the Americans on defense. (Their defense budget represented 11 percent of their GNP as compared with the American's 5 percent.) "Clearly," writes Mr. Ross, drawing the only possible conclusion, "the Soviet Union and other Communist nations are able to maintain larger and growing military forces, while investing in ambitious development programs, only because they can borrow from the West. Every dollar they borrow for trade and development releases an equivalent amount of regular domestic revenue for military use." And he goes on to suggest, most convincingly, that in the future credit should be linked to disarmament.

Here I would agree with him wholeheartedly. If we are to give the Russians credit, we must make quite sure that we get something worth having in return, and there can be no doubt that a genuine and substantial reduction in the present enormous volume of Soviet armaments would do something to reduce the threat they at present represent to world peace. Indeed, if this were on a sufficient scale, it might even make possible a measure of Western disarmament in return, in itself a desirable development. On the other hand, for the Western powers to go out of their way to make it easier for the Russians to build up their armed strength still further for eventual use against us must be sheer lunacy. And, as Mr. Ross himself says, the sooner this is generally realized and the necessary conclusions drawn, the better.

Looking into the future, the author would like to see the United States making use of its financial, economic, and technological strength to achieve a measure of active cooperation with Russia and China in the economic field, regardless of ideological differences and divergencies. Large scale credits would be granted to the Russians in return for a dramatic reduction in armaments and to the Chinese in return for shelving the question of Taiwan. "Today," he writes, "technology and trade link the power centers of the planet." And he comes back to his theme of interdependence and to the enormous increase there could be in world prosperity were less money spent on armaments.

In assessing the world situation, it is important not to underestimate, as a factor in international affairs, the force of the Soviet drive for world domination nor, for that matter, the armed might of the Soviet Union at the present time. On the other hand, provided the Western powers pursue a completely realistic policy, provided they have the courage of their convictions and do not for an instant lower their guard, either politically or militarily, provided above all that they remain strong, I do not myself see why something of the kind envisaged by Mr. Ross might not eventually come about. The balance of terror (so long as it is properly maintained) makes a third world war unlikely. Both Russia and China are gradually opening up more and more to outside influences. Both are evolving. There are even signs in both of an emergent public opinion. With luck, both may some day become less difficult to live with. Nor can it be denied that trade and technology are powerful catalysts. The danger, of course, lies in any weakening on the part of the West either militarily or ideologically. This, if it went too far, could well convince the Russians that the moment had arrived for a trial of strength and, whichever way that went, it would clearly put to rest all dreams of peace and prosperity in our lifetime and well beyond it.

Argyll, Scotland   F. M.
July 1978

1
THE MULTINATIONAL CORPORATIONS

One of the outstanding international trends of the 1960s was the rapid growth of the multinational corporation. Neither the World Bank nor the International Monetary Fund was as active then as it is today. Multinational corporations provided the main conduit through which capital from one country was invested in another—an inescapable step toward the achievement of accelerated development.

The scarcity of alternative development funds, however, inevitably created a dependency on the multinationals, which was naturally resented by countries seeking capital. Furthermore, the unfettered power of the multinationals led to abuses—ranging from the manipulation of international currency flows to bribery and pollution. Consequently, a mounting clamor of criticism, some of it justified, faced the multinationals when the first of these three papers was presented, in September 1971. The United Nations was, in fact, preparing to convene a special session of the General Assembly to deal with the problems presented by the multinationals and the imbalance in the world economy.

The following three papers were written as a frank

response to those criticisms, in the belief that the multinationals, if properly regulated, offered the best — if not the only — means of providing needed development at that time.

Recent events have changed the picture to some degree. The collapse of commodity prices, and the increase in energy costs since the OPEC oil embargo, slowed down global growth and the growth of the multinational corporation. Moreover, the IMF, the World Bank, and the regional development agencies are offering alternative sources of development funding, and it now seems generally recognized that the imbalances in the world economy can best be righted through such multilateral operations.

Some of the constant, intense criticism of the multinationals has therefore subsided, although the corporations remain a potent and growing force still largely unrestrained. However, as noted in the third paper, "The Role of the Multinational Corporation in Global Affairs," some steps toward regulating the multinationals are now being taken, but much remains to be done.

THE MULTINATIONAL CORPORATION IN THE GRAND DESIGN OF INTERNATIONALISM

(1971)

An outline of the history and importance of multinational corporations....Citing and responding to some of the criticisms of them. ...Pointing out that the profit motive, although conducive to business efficiency, does not guarantee the achievement of social objectives....Enumerating some of the multinationals' responsibilities and opportunities....Suggesting that NATO should establish a code of rules to govern them.

The multinational corporation has become rather suddenly a major topic of controversy in politics and economics. One fact that appears beyond dispute is the profound influence that those corporations exercise on world affairs through their producing and distributing patterns. Their estimated output is already almost one-sixth of total world production, and one-fourth of the total for the Western world alone. Moreover, with a growth rate faster than national economic growth rates, the international companies are obtaining a steadily increasing share of world output and are internationalizing a vast sector of world production. This output, estimated as larger than any national economy other than the United States, represents an emerging sector that in the aggregate is close to reaching a critical mass that would make the world's output basically and irreversibly international.

If controlled and directed constructively, with a high

Paper presented to the Political and Economic Committees. North Atlantic Assembly. Ottawa, September 1971.

sense of humanism, these international corporations can bring about stability and prosperity; they can help create order out of confusion. But if indifferent to consumer needs, if operated without social objectives or government restraints, and if dominated exclusively by the profit motive, these same entities will set back the potential human benefit of the free enterprise system more than they advance it.

The corporation is simply an invention of man that forges the skills of people into an instrument of production. As such, the multinational corporations are, potentially, peerless forces for benefit in a world much of which is gripped in poverty. They provide the means for unifying and reconciling the aspirations of the world's population—a task which statesmen and politicians have utterly failed to achieve.

Assuring that this potential is realized is a major political and economic challenge of our time. Social decisions must be brought into play consciously to meet human needs. The profit motive alone is not enough to assure conformance to local regulations and traditions, nor the broadest possible use of local personnel, not to say good and safe products at fair prices. This is a world problem, more soluble by international means. It is, particularly, a challenge to the NATO countries, as Western Europe and the United States account for most of the new patterns of internationalized production.

Size and Scope of International Investment

Just how big are the multinational, or international, corporations—that is, companies that produce and sell in more than one country? The best way to trace their growth is to examine the data on international investment. In brief, the total of U.S. investment abroad, government and private taken together, expanded from a base point of $32 billion in 1950 to $146 billion in the two decades following. Of these totals, direct private in-

24

vestment—mainly through overseas branches and subsidiaries of U.S. multinational companies—accounted for one-third of the total in 1950, growing to nearly one-half in the next two decades.

In the same period, other countries' investments in the United States grew from $18 billion to $91 billion, most of which was in short-term and portfolio investments. Direct private investment in the United States by foreign-based multinational companies makes up less than one-seventh of the total foreign investment in the United States.

There are a number of arresting features of this basic investment structure:

● Its rapid growth—more than nine percent a year, or twice as fast as general economic growth.

● For the United States, the strong central position of direct investment by its international or multinational companies with branches and subsidiaries in various countries.

● The lesser scale but strong growth of other countries' investment in the U.S. market. Here the pattern is the reverse of U.S. investment in terms of maturities and risk. More than half is in short-term assets, which reflects (a) the scale of foreign banking in America; (b) the growth of the Euro-dollar market as the centerpiece of international financing; (c) the structurally related U.S. balance-of-payments deficits which leave surplus dollars in foreign hands; and (d) the traditional strong liquidity preference of foreign investors.

The Magnitude of Production

A great deal is known about the volume of output associated with these investments. The annual sales of foreign subsidiaries of U.S. international companies can be estimated at double the direct investment figures. Output associated with other kinds of investment presumably involves a lower factor than the two-to-one ratio appropriate for direct investment. Although the basis for estimating is concededly not firm, a one-to-one ratio seems plausible. For example, if banks perform their basic function of intermediating short-term deposits into productive investment, an equal amount of output seems a relatively conservative inference for a year's employment of funds. Assuming the same impact for portfolio and all other nondirect categories of investment combined, the total output comes to about $217 billion, not including the sales of international companies in their home markets.

It is noteworthy that this figure for the sales value of American activities abroad is almost five times larger than traditional U.S. exports. Thus, for every dollar of goods and services furnished foreign markets through exports, there are five dollars furnished through operations abroad.

Similar analysis of foreigners' investment activities in the United States and elsewhere in the world leads to a broad estimate of a roughly equal level of output, resulting in a grand total of $450 billion of 1969 production attributed to international investment.

Output of $450 billion represents nearly one-sixth of estimated gross world production of $3 trillion. It is half again larger than the entire volume of world exports. This $450 billion is almost entirely the output of NATO-area companies, and it exceeds the estimated $350 billion output of all the less-developed countries combined.

Thus, $450 billion in product seems to represent a "critical mass" presaging an international production explosion. At a growth rate of eight percent, a rate conservatively below the 1950–1969 experience, this production would double by 1979, at which time it becomes about a fifth rather than a sixth of world output and within fifty years, fully half. So we are in fact committed to a system not only of international trade but also of international production.

26

How Did the New International System Come About?

Many factors contributed to the accelerated pace of international investment after World War II. The first was the general economic situation of the European NATO countries at that time: destroyed and disrupted productive facilities were inevitably accompanied by gravely impaired foreign-exchange resources. (For quite different reasons, the condition roughly paralleled the familiar low-productivity position of less-developed countries.) Foreign-exchange reserves and earnings were strictly budgeted under policies aimed at keeping consumer imports to the essential minimum and at providing as large an amount of producers' goods as possible.

Foreign investment was everywhere welcome to augment scarce local resources. The barriers against nonessential imports confronted foreign suppliers with a situation in which their traditional markets could be maintained only by producing locally. Moreover, in most countries, foreign companies' earnings were blocked and investment became the best available use for the funds. To encourage local production and attract more capital, most countries began liberalizing the remittance of earning.

Another basic factor contributing to the accelerating pace of international investment was the elevation of European demand to a point where the large-scale producing methods of American industry became appropriate. The buoyancy of demand imposed profit prospects, and economic development invited the application of advanced industrial technology. The European productive surge by the mid-1950s created conditions favorable to the unification of Western European markets into the Common Market, and the subsequent tariff reductions contributed to a further surge of production. Active American investment accelerated from the late 1950s on, especially in European manufacturing.

Investment in the United Kingdom gave access to the European Free Trade Association, with its sophisticated population of 100 million consumers.

Above all, the rapid and dramatic improvement in world communications removed the old boundaries that separated traditional markets. International telephone circuits and communications satellites assure virtually instant sound and visual contact throughout the world, thus creating a new, enlarged world community.

Criticism of Multinational Corporations

Hostile criticism of international companies is extensive—and often deserved. When raised to the level of international affairs, the potential of companies to behave selfishly and without regard to human social objectives becomes unlimited. The discrepancy between the global range of corporate operations and the monitoring range of corresponding political authorities leads to serious problems. There are no world regulatory agencies, or registration and taxing authorities, or fair practice and labor standards, or tribunals to deal with conflicts of law or any agencies to force the multinationals to meet predetermined social obligations.

Among the frequent criticisms are the following:

Subsidiaries to a large extent carry out the policies of their parent. These policies are influenced by the home government and are frequently at odds with locally desired goals and with the national policies of the host countries. This is particularly true in the financial sphere: international banking may frustrate a host country's financial policies on interest rates, prices, costs, the business cycle, economic development, and similar matters.

In order to maximize profits, companies impose economic straitjackets on the development potential of poorer countries, exploiting local resources for the benefit of outsiders.

Given the scale of their operations and all too little regulation, the multinationals have become, inadvertently, major polluters of the environment.

The mere size of international companies makes effective new competition more difficult. Through growth and mergers, various critical sectors of world production and finance are gradually drifting into the hands of relatively few companies.

Thus it is clear that political and social controls have not kept pace with our economic instruments.

Shortcomings of the Multinational Corporate Network

Analysis of the total world output ("World GNP") by region during this period makes it apparent that the interproducing network is overwhelmingly concentrated in the NATO group. Approximately one-third of the total world output is accounted for by the United States, and another one-third by the other developed countries of the West (with Japan included). The remaining one-third is divided roughly as follows: 17 percent for the East Bloc, including the USSR; 12 percent for the less-developed countries; and about 4 percent for China. The challenge before us is to spread the network into these other areas.

Relations with the Less-Developed Countries

The industrial ties between the developed and less-developed countries are sketchy and highly specialized. At the moment they are weakening in Latin America, most of Africa, Southeast Asia, and the Indian subcontinent. The international system has not brought the less-developed countries into the Western economic fabric of high productivity per capita, which is essential for orderly development.

The less-developed countries, aware of the specialized character of help available from abroad, decry it for depleting their raw materials to benefit the more developed world and for freezing their economies into a mold of relative poverty. With rare and special exceptions—for example, Israel and Taiwan, and another group of countries such as Saudi Arabia, Kuwait, and Libya for other, obvious, special reasons—less-developed countries do not progress into the world of decent per-capita income. Almost without exception the less-developed countries believe that the private companies and the free enterprise system of the industrialized world are incapable of changing their situation. They believe, rightly or wrongly, that the limitations imposed by history, climate, and geography present no insuperable obstacle. The multinational, concentrating on raw material production, hesitates to carry out intermediate and final manufacturing processes in the developing countries. This caution comes from the risk involved in establishing capital-intensive activities in areas of political instability or in countries having different economic and social systems. The reluctance is understandable but the gap thus created brings about an untenable disparity of standards.

Stronger undertakings between the host countries and the multinational corporations are needed to protect their separate concerns and release the mainsprings of progress. But this seems to await the establishment of an international body that will promulgate criteria and wield enforcement powers.

Relations with the East Bloc

The imbalance between the economies of the West and those of the Soviet bloc countries and China is primarily political in nature. Minor technical difficulties— such as finding common denominators of trade, production, and finance between the government-planned production of the East and the private market system of the West—could be readily overcome. Dramatic progress could be made if the arbitrary barriers of political differences were torn down. (See "The Ties That Bind," page 132.)

It is possible to conceive of an increasingly integrated Western world of highly developed economies alongside two other separate worlds, one primarily Communist-oriented politically and economically, and one of underdevelopment. But the West's highly interdependent system of production more and more both illustrates and suggests a world society whose efficiency depends on the best allocation of resources on a global basis. In fact, some integration between the Eastern bloc and the West has already been accomplished by innovative projects such as the pipelines that knit together Russia and Western Europe. Economics is the interplay of competing opportunities for the use of resources. Those opportunities are no less real as they occur in Western, Eastern, or Third World areas. Politics may complicate economics but can rarely nullify it. The relative weight of politics and economics seems slowly but surely to be shifting in favor of the latter.

Lack of Ecology Controls

A third shortcoming of the emerging international system is its failure to assure the integrity of the planet's resources. Matter is not created or destroyed, but the acts of transformation produce residues that are passed off into the air and water streams of the planet or are left to litter the landscape. This is an old observation and applies to man's "transforming" operations from the beginning of time. What is new to the twentieth century is the realization that our level of transformation is now yielding such a high volume of effluents that the air and water streams can no longer carry them off and distribute them innocuously.

Beyond this, very perplexing questions have arisen as to whether world resources can be extended by present Western-type technology to the less-developed countries. The basic materials of the planet are finite. Known

31

reserves do not permit the extension of per capita consumption at, say, the U.S. level to an indefinitely growing world population.

These are but illustrative comments. A proper husbanding of planetary resources, the revolutionizing of recycling, the reduction of pollution to levels consistent with the vital processes of the planet—these necessary efforts all fall outside of the accounting systems of companies and, so far, of nations, too. These environmental considerations will require more and more activity at every level of social organization. The basic problem is world-wide; it will call for world analysis, and it will become a charge on world resources. The international companies, instead of resisting, must play a leading role in identifying the specific problems, in suggesting the most practical solutions, and in providing business leadership to make agreed programs effective.

Surely the protection of people and resources menaced by careless processing is an urgent defense problem which the NATO group is well equipped to analyze and address. Finally, because of the competitive nature of the free enterprise system, governments, or better yet, the United Nations must establish clear, workable guidelines. (See "The Role of the Multinational Corporation in Global Affairs," page 43.)

A Constructive Step for NATO

The NATO countries constitute the very core of world production and the international money and capital markets. In all these matters NATO has a concern and a potential for action. I recommend that the North Atlantic Assembly begin an orderly examination of the problems of international investment and production with these objectives:

- To suggest means of reducing the barriers to production and trade between East and West.
- To determine the feasibility of establishing, with all

the governments concerned, a judicial tribunal and a code of rules covering the rights and obligations of host countries and of the multinational corporations that wish to operate within them.

● To make appropriate recommendations in dealing with ecological factors in the production cycle.

● To study the investment of NATO countries in the underdeveloped world. All countries should be encouraged to develop more comparable accounting information on capital movements and foreign investment. A program should be established to determine the timeliness and scope of a NATO investment advisory commission to keep this work current and to suggest needed work by other international bodies.

The multinational corporations now operate at a global level made possible by our industrial, commercial, and communications technology. They have created an international force of great dynamism and efficiency, and are in a position, when their objectives include ecological, social, and humanistic goals, to play a central role in a vast and creative effort to benefit mankind. If they choose not to, they will become a legitimate target for governmental attack and paralyzing over-regulation. ◉

Postscript

Since this report was presented in 1971, both the world economy and the operations of the multinational corporations have indeed expanded remarkably. Increases in energy costs have so far prevented an explosive growth quite as large as was expected. "World GNP" has more than doubled and is now estimated at over $6 trillion. More than one-sixth can probably be attributed to international production as described in this paper.

Assuming that foreign investment activity in the United States still bears approximately the same ratio to foreign investment activity world-wide as it did in 1969, production attributable to international investment has reached more than $950 billion in the present decade. Output associated with U.S. international investments alone has gone over the $420 billion mark. (None of these figures has been adjusted for inflation.)

The Multinational Corporations

The increase in OPEC oil revenues has also drastically increased the proportion of short-term foreign investment in the United States. While direct foreign investment in the United States grew from $12 billion to $30 billion between 1969 and 1976, short-term foreign government investments were increasing from $19 billion to $106 billion — much of it oil profits seeking a safe haven.

Disappointingly, NATO has not become involved in the study of international investment and production as was urged by the author, but the United Nations has, as decribed in "The Role of the Multinational Corporation in Global Affairs," page 43.

SOCIAL IMPLICATIONS OF BUSINESS CONCENTRATION

(1973)

A deeper examination of the problems that arise as economic power is concentrated, particularly the difficulties governments face in controlling corporate growth in order to avoid social and environmental damage ....Concluding with a plea for better regulation of multinationals.

One hears a great deal these days—and usually in strident terms—about the increasing concentration of power in multinational corporations and the social implications of this concentration. Certainly, multinational companies provide unequivocal examples of massive economic power, and it is impossible to divorce economic power from political power. Our concerns here, however, are first to examine how and why such business concentrations evolved, second, what these trends seem to suggest for the future, and, finally, the social consequences of concentration.

Helpful Approach

A useful analytical approach to business concentration, one with a great deal of relevance to a variety of current problems, is the theory of economies and diseconomies of scale. Very briefly, the theory tells us that a corporation gains advantages, termed "economies of scale," as its operations grow: expansion encourages specialization of labor and management, the utilization of more productive equipment, and similar economies,

Originally published in the Magazine of the Gottlieb Duttweiler Institute. Zurich, February 1973.

all of which increase efficiency and permit the firm to lower its product price. Thus in the final stages of this theory, both the corporation and the public benefit from growth.

But after a time the firm may become so large that it suffers from its size. Coordination of production processes becomes much more costly than before. These "diseconomies of scale" naturally lead to inefficiencies and result in higher product prices.

The theory of economies and diseconomies of scale presents an obvious dilemma: growth is beneficial up to a point, after which it is not; but where is that point? The answer is tautological: Whenever diseconomies of scale begin to outweigh economies, further expansion becomes counter-productive for all concerned.

Economies of scale affected the post-war development of international investment and production. In their efforts to rebuild domestic productive capacities, European governments not only restricted all nonessential imports, but also discouraged their own citizens from investing elsewhere while encouraging foreigners to invest in their countries. The multinational companies, which actually did the investing, took full advantage of the economies of scale made possible by international production and markets. Moreover, these companies were aided by the then-new international regulatory agencies, such as the IMF and GATT, which freed them from most of the traditional restrictions of territorial jurisdiction and enabled them to move human, technological, and natural resources around the globe in pursuit of their goals.

Current Trends in Multinationals

This process has continued, and we now speak accurately of a "world economy" in which the very structures of production and distribution are internationalized, as is the ancillary banking network. We might note in passing that much of the trouble we are now experiencing with our international payments system is the result of the fact that national governments have yet to accommodate themselves fully to the already internationalized production and banking structures.

The size and scope of the multinational corporations are impressive. Of the world's one hundred largest entities—in terms of employment, assets, annual budgets, and expenditures—fifty-nine, expectably, are national governments. But the other forty-one, remarkably, are multinational corporations.

These figures indicate, among other things, that the world cannot afford a return to simple patterns of domestic production or investment, despite the fondest dreams of protectionists. More important, there are a variety of developments within multinational corporations that have important consequences. It is apparent, for example, that definitions like "foreign" and "domestic" are increasingly meaningless in international economic life. Multinational companies are not the exclusive preserve of any particular nation, no matter where their headquarters may be located. By the same token, corporate decision-making is not the exclusive preserve of certain national executives but is itself increasingly an internationalized process.

Great companies learned some time ago that absolute concentration in decision-making would not work and it was an expensive lesson to learn in many cases. One example of this is the Ford Motor Company, which, under the one-man dominance of Harry Bennett, nearly collapsed, showing a profit only once (1932) in the twenty-year span from 1927–1947. Local production has meant local participation in decision-making, and national governments no longer permit local investment that does not significantly involve their own nationals. This is a healthy and inevitable arrangement.

Finally, multinationals, although enormous in every respect, are not monolithic. Essentially and increasingly, they operate as structures of autonomous parts in a corporate whole, making assessments and decisions that respond to local conditions while at the same time gaining efficiency by acting through the whole corporate apparatus. Probably General Motors first initiated this process of decentralization on a large scale when it reorganized into divisions that were allowed to compete with each other in order to innovate and maintain efficiency and to capture different automobile "markets," that is, the market for luxury cars, for family cars, and for trucks. The decentralization process has continued and spread internationally, so that today multinational corporations increasingly reflect a kind of "diversity in unity" in their various activities.

World Integration Through Economic Dependence

We now stand on the threshold of a new era of international interdependence. The financiers and the industrialists, along with their international lawyers, have knit the world together by vast movements of goods and services. Vessels leave daily from the great seaports of the western hemisphere carrying an immense volume of agricultural products to be unloaded in regular procession at leading ports in the eastern hemisphere, thus making huge and widely disparate populations dependent on each other. Vast deposits of oil and gas presently locked in remote areas of Alaska and Siberia will be moved eastward and westward by pipeline and tanker to the East and West coasts of the United States and will provide these areas with energy and heat and the sinews of life.

These immense projects, to be brought about by economic pressures and carried out by the business sector of our society under government supervision, could significantly reduce the need for substantial military expenditures by all governments. The game of power politics played by world political leaders and diplomats, which has resulted in the disastrous sacrifice of tens of millions of human beings, could be made to yield to international economic imperatives. Governments, as the proponents of varying and competing ideologies and political concepts, will have a far lesser role to play then heretofore.

These trends, however, will further concentrate business decisions. That, in turn, will make more necessary the role of governments and international regulatory agencies in order to control the social consequences of these programs.

Social Limits to Growth

The world has become obsessed with the notion that growth is good. Indeed, so pervasive is this idea that its orthodoxy goes largely unquestioned, and those who do dissent are dismissed as unrealistic. The GNP, which is really nothing more than an arithmetical counting system, is idolized as a kind of economic golden calf. But we are suffering from the ill effects of industrial growth unchecked by social considerations and it is now clear that we cannot really progress without adequate social controls on growth.

We once left to natural economic laws the limitations to the growth of concentration. Our very old Adam Smithian assumption was that whenever any corporation reached the limit of its profitable growth, the marketplace would apply the brakes to further expansion by shifting consumer demand to more efficiently organized competitors. We now have found, however, that this natural law takes too long to operate, resulting in an erosion of the social and economic structure of the free-enterprise system. Thus the system requires government supervision that is both enlightened about the advantages of the competitive free-enterprise system and sufficiently socially conscious to respond to the needs of society as a whole.

It is my opinion that the failure so far to set adequate social limitations to growth is due largely to one essential fact: although economies of scale have enormously aided the growth of international production and are meticulously accounted for, corresponding "social diseconomies of scale"—meaning here pollutions of all kinds, both social and environmental—have either "escaped" our accounting systems or, which seems more probable, simply have never been admitted. All kinds of destructive activities that cost society real resources are never adequately assessed. To take a particularly perverse example, the vast sums that change hands annually in the international narcotics trade, for instance, are nowhere entered into GNP accounts.

At the risk of sounding anticapitalist, which I certainly am not, I cite a few other current examples of our inability to reckon with "diseconomies." We are capable of devising intricate formulae to calculate plant and equipment depreciation, but none for housing deterioration. Yet every year millions of dwelling units become uninhabitable slums all over the world. Every new automobile that rolls off the Detroit assembly lines figures into GNP computations, but never the pollution these cars will certainly produce; nor, for that matter, will there be any assessment for the thousands of lives lost annually in automobile accidents, unless it be that for funeral expenses.

Clearly the fault does not lie in our institutional devices themselves but in the fact that we systematically exclude these gross social diseconomies from our accounting systems. In choosing to have a system of private automobile transportation we are implicitly choosing also to have air pollution, a paved-over countryside, and the death or maiming of tens of thousands annually in inevitable traffic accidents. In choosing the "more efficient" production methods we also choose, for example, strip-mining extraction, which may in some sense be "cheaper," but which desecrates the landscape. In choosing to maintain a "defense" establishment that

40

gobbles up an excessive share of all governmental resources, we also choose to deprive ourselves of mass transportation systems, urban renewal, better medical facilities, and many other kinds of necessary government services.

It is commonly claimed that there is no adequate way to measure the many types of social diseconomies. A typical example of measurement problems is that while the smoke discharge from a plant may be irritating or even deadly, it cannot be economically measured and therefore cannot be properly accounted for. This may be so, but as a start, one might compute the costs of laundry, window cleaning, and lung medication in the locality and charge it to the offending plant until smoke controls are installed. Of course, such a suggestion is made in jest, but the essential point is that measurements, however approximate, should be devised.

Theoretically, the government regulates and taxes in order to control the harmful effects of social diseconomies. For the most part, and unfortunately, governments everywhere do not respond to these problems adequately. To cite but one illustrative example, there is an obvious need for low-income housing in most countries, but little is being done to construct it. Yet one views with amazement the high-rise luxury condominiums being constructed around the world, often within sight of the most squalid slums.

The GNP reflects the condominium construction but ignores the lack of low-cost housing because those in need of the latter have not the market muscle to bring about its development. This social deficiency, which can lead to revolution, is further masked by a rising GNP index.

Summary

The real danger of concentration in any form, economic or otherwise, is that it constitutes great power, and as everyone now knows, power tends to corrupt. This concentration of economic power has been enormously beneficial in providing mankind with material wealth but the wealth has not been adequately distributed and the social consequences have not been calculated. Being an optimist, I would say that our system, having always managed to respond to new challenges in the past, will find ways of doing so again and will meet these new requirements. But the time is short, and the needs are great. ◉

THE ROLE OF THE MULTINATIONAL CORPORATION IN GLOBAL AFFAIRS

(1975)

> *The history of multinationals in greater detail. ...Pointing out that many modern technological developments originated outside of the United States and that multinationals spread these developments throughout the world .... Describing a new epoch for multinationals, beginning with specific developments in 1974 that provided blueprints for regulating the multinational corporations.*

The growth of multinational corporations was heralded as the dawn of a new era of international prosperity and improvement in economic conditions around the globe. These same advances have more recently been viewed suspiciously in many quarters as posing a threat to national sovereignties, and as evidence of international oligopoly.

There have certainly been many abuses. But many of these excesses are on the way to rapid correction. We should not lose ourselves in the rhetoric of the past and rail against problems that either no longer exist or that are being solved by a new awareness and newly created safeguards. It is crucial to consider the subject from the historical perspective and see both what the record indicates and what it holds for the future.

Historical Perspective

The attempt to move goods and services through the world was one of the earliest of man's endeavors and

Address to students of the Wharton Entrepreneurial Center, The Wharton School, University of Pennsylvania. Philadelphia, November 6, 1975.

43

continues to this day. Perhaps the first real international trading effort, the forerunner of today's multinational corporation, occurred some 2,000 years ago when a caravan of camels struggled to its feet outside one of China's great cities. Laden with silks and spices, this caravan wended its way through the Great Gobi Desert, the Middle East, North Africa, across the Sahara, and on to Timbuktu and West Africa. The caravan had its upstream sources of supply and its downstream distributors, not unlike the multinationals of today.

Eventually, the caravans were followed by the great sailing and oar-propelled fleets of the Phoenicians, carrying rugs, metalware, and other goods from the Levant for distribution throughout the countries of the Mediterranean basin.

By the seventeenth and eighteenth centuries, English jurisprudence had given birth to that ingenious and creative mechanism, the corporation. It was endowed with immortality and an existence independent of the men who controlled and directed its affairs. This legal instrument released powerful forces into history.

A corporation is, in a sense, an institution created to combine the skills of man with the resources of the earth for productive purposes. It has the potential of providing a flexible and useful vehicle for the circulation of socioeconomic knowledge and benefits throughout the world.

The adventurous men of the seventeenth and eighteenth centuries formed such legendary concerns as the East India Company, Massachusetts Bay Company, and—to use the exact title—the Governor and Company of Adventurers of England Trading into Hudson's Bay— otherwise known as the Hudson Bay Company. These and others were to alter the course of history.

The Multinational Corporation in the Colonial Period

Throughout most of the nineteenth century, the development of international companies was synonymous with the building of the great European colonial empires. Continents were carved up in fierce competition both for raw materials to fuel the European industrial revolution and to provide markets for European industrial products. English, French, German, and Dutch companies followed—and in some cases led—their flags around the world, linking remote places to their metropolitan centers. In the process, ports were constructed, railroads laid, canals dug, and telegraph wires strung—all by companies.

We have only to think of the building of the Suez Canal to recall the close link between company affairs and international politics. The Suez Canal was constructed by the brilliant and resourceful Ferdinand de Lesseps under the auspices of a French stock company, which sold shares on the Paris bourse to finance the project. When the ruling Khedive of Egypt found himself financially embarrassed, he negotiated the sale of his controlling shares to the British government in 1875, thus initiating British control over Egypt. The matter was handled by Prime Minister Disraeli for an appreciative Queen Victoria.

1900—1945: The First Epoch of the Modern Multinational Corporation

The first great modern epoch in the evolution of the multinationals may be thought of as occurring in the first half of this century. Like the colonial period before it, this period was marked by a continued search for markets and raw materials, but it witnessed something new: the emergence of American companies into the international sphere. Prior to 1900, and early in this new modern period, U.S. companies in general followed the domestic westward expansion of the country and did not venture outside our borders. Later in this period U.S. companies did go abroad, but not aggressively until after World War II. After all, in the long view, the United States itself was a developing country until the mid-twentieth century. It was preoccupied with its own development and the absorption of the new European technologies.

The 1900–1945 phase was, as I have noted, mainly a continuation of the search for raw materials to meet the needs of the industrial world—for the tin of Bolivia, the copper of Chile and Zambia, bauxite of Jamaica and Guyana, tropical fruits of Central America, sugar of the West Indies, rubber of Malaysia and Brazil, and the oil of Indonesia and the Middle East, to name but a few.

During this initial phase, the multinational companies were generally not aggressive in establishing manufacturing facilities in foreign lands. Rather, these early efforts were characterized by the explorations of adventurers appearing on the shores of previously unnoticed, little-developed parts of the world and attempting to obtain raw materials from these areas and deliver them to the markets of the West.

1945—1973: The Second Epoch

The next great epoch in the multinational evolution took place after World War II. Its hallmark, the establishment of manufacturing facilities in a host country, received a great impetus from the necessity to rebuild the war-torn European economies. Foreign exporters could only maintain their European markets by producing locally.

It was in this environment that the Marshall Plan was launched in 1948 to further facilitate both governmental and private investments in Europe. The Marshall Plan had far-reaching consequences. By 1951 its coordinating influence would lead directly to Jean Monnet's European Coal and Steel Community and only six years later, in 1957, to the Treaty of Rome and the European Economic Community.

In the less developed areas of the world, economic planners of many persuasions witnessed the miraculous recovery of Europe and came to believe that corporate investments in productive facilities in their own countries would spell success there too. Thus, governments of developing countries everywhere outbid one another to attract corporations, offering favorable tax and tariff regulations and other inducements.

A massive wave of multinational investment spread across the globe in the 1950s and 1960s. So vast have those investments been that we now speak meaningfully of an "International Economy," representing international production that aggregates some $500 billion of goods and services and that has committed the world to a system of international trade.

It appears probable that the process of internationalization of production will continue, thus assisting the developing countries in their struggle to improve living standards. In 1957, for example, U.S. companies were investing about nine cents of every dollar expended overseas on new plant and equipment. By 1971, this portion had risen to twenty-five cents of every dollar invested in new plant and equipment. In 1961, the sales of all American manufacturing subsidiaries abroad represented only 7 percent of total U.S. sales, but by 1971, foreign sales accounted for 13 percent of the total sales of all U.S. manufacturing companies [and around 25% in 1977]. And of course similar trends exist for the multinational corporations of foreign countries. These figures indicate the healthy trend toward increased international investment and production.

An American Monopoly?

In this country we somehow have come to regard the multinational as a peculiarly American entity. But multinationals are global in origin as well as in scope. Royal Dutch Shell, Ericsson Telephones, Lever

Brothers, Philips Lamp, Imperial Chemicals, Siemens Halske, Brown Boveri, Hoffmann LaRoche, Mannesman Steel, and Tokyo Fire & Marine—all are global concerns. The world's biggest operating branch bank system, for example, is Britain's National Westminster, with some 3,500 branches and offices on all the continents; our own largest international bank, Citicorp, has about 1,900 branches and offices worldwide. The reach of the great Japanese companies—Mitsubishi, Mitsui, Sumitomo, Hitachi, and others—is by now legendary. Their growth is even more remarkable considering the low state of the Japanese economy after World War II. Competition is fierce among these giants, and an opportunity overlooked by one will be seized upon by another.

Everyone knows that Europeans invented or discovered the steam engine, electricity, the electric motor, electric transmission, radioactivity (with the resulting world of X-rays), internal combustion cycles (with the resulting gasoline and diesel engines), the synthesis of ammonia, synthetic dyes, and pharmaceuticals—the list can go on and on. It might be said that these developments, after all, occurred in a by-gone age and that we in America now have all the new knowledge and science and technology, but actually that is not quite the case.

Consider, for example, some of the important new technologies that have emerged since World War II.

● Atomic Energy: An American contribution? Hardly. The seminal thinkers were Einstein and Heisenberg, both Germans, Fermi, an Italian, and Rutherford, an Englishman. Americans such as Oppenheimer, Lawrence, and Urey helped mainly with the subsequent technology.

● Antibiotics: Are those remarkable life savers American? Indeed not. British science: in this case, Sir Alexander Fleming.

● Rocketry: This has made possible our first escape from this planet, moon exploration, and tomorrow's interplanetary exploration. This work was entirely of

German origin.

● Aviation: With American-built 600-mph jet planes nearly monopolizing the world aircraft market, surely they must be the result of American science and technology. Actually, not quite true. The heart of it all, the turbine engine, was a British contribution during World War II; Sir Frank Whittle was the prime developer.

Well, all right, we may say, some others did help with the basic science, but American products and business methods now monopolize the world through American multinational companies, and what goes forth to the world from abroad is minimal. Again, a caution! When an American traveler goes elsewhere in the world he takes for granted that he will see Ford and Firestone, Coca-Cola, IBM, and Polaroid. But he may forget that prestigious names come from subsidiaries of foreign companies: Sony and Philips, Toyota, Volkswagen, Shell, Olivetti, Rolls-Royce, Leica, or Ericsson Telephone.

The dramatic technological developments that have taken place in communications and transportation in the past thirty years cannot be kept at home in their countries of origin. Communication cannot be stifled; it has fired and fueled the revolution of rising expectations.

The point is that the U.S.A., big and powerful and dominant as it is today, was, only a moment ago in history, a member of the developing world, importing the technologies and mores of Europe. We still are only one member of this larger society which, through the mundane day-to-day business of corporate competition, helps to bring the whole family of man up to date with the current state of knowledge and technology.

Whatever the reasons may be, the capacity to serve the revolution of rising expectations that has swept through the world and its 138 UN members rests primarily with the multinational corporations of Western Europe, the United States, and Japan. It is a simple fact that other nations or blocs devoted to different types of political and economic structures have not participated to the same degree, if at all, in the delivery to the rest of the world of the great new technologies that have been developed on this globe during this century. The Soviet Union, for example, of course had to be a late starter with the devastation of World War II and its primitive conditions before that. On the other hand Japan started with just as little in the decade of the '50s, but its multinationals have delivered much to the developing world and improved the standards of living of people everywhere.

I have already pointed out that China was possibly the first to launch the multinational concept with its great camel caravans of 2,000 years ago. In its own historic evolution, however, China has hardly played a role in the improvement of the living conditions of the people of the earth or in the worldwide distribution of the new technologies of the last few hundred years.

This is not to deprecate one system as against another. It is simply to say that the apparatus for transmitting the great technologies throughout the world resides primarily with the multinationals of the developed capitalist world.

Criticisms of Multinationals

Early in 1975, *the New Yorker* published a series of notable articles on the multinational corporation. One of the main criticisms in the articles was that multinationals were exploiting foreign labor markets and were exporting jobs to remote areas of the world at the expense of domestic labor. This criticism, of course, could be as applicable to foreign-based multinationals as to our own.

I regard this argument as considerably distorted. First, the establishment of a foreign-based plant creates jobs and payrolls, transfers technology, provides tax revenues, and creates foreign exchange in other areas of the world. This reflects one of the great contributions of the multinationals. Moreover, it would be erroneous for anyone to assume, for example, that RCA could preserve jobs by not moving an existing plant from Peoria, Illinois, let us say, to Taiwan, where production costs are lower. Be assured that if RCA does not move this plant, Philips Lamp of The Netherlands will build a plant in Taiwan and bring the product to Illinois, forcing an RCA closing in any event. This is the competitive system, producing products for human needs at the lowest cost to the benefit of all. Were it not for this interplay it would be literally impossible to integrate the developing countries into the international economic system.

As for wages paid by the large corporations in the developing world, these are naturally and inevitably lower than those in the more mature societies. Nevertheless, these wages usually are among the highest prevailing in a host country because of the skilled workers involved. Apart from the fact that these wages are always subject to government control, they are, in reality, set by the economic environment of the host country. It would be a most dangerous and unwelcome step if the wages paid were out of all proportion to, let us say, what the government could pay its employees or what other manufacturers could support by local endeavors.

Multinational employment figures are indeed impressive. To note but a few: Royal Dutch Shell's 1973 year-end employment was 168,000, for which wage and social compensation expenses totaled over $2 billion; Philips Lamp employed some 371,000 people, of which fewer than a third (97,000) were in The Netherlands; Lever Brothers employs 353,000 people around the globe; while Siemens Halske employs 305,000.

In the United States, according to a recent Commerce Department study, U.S. multinationals' domestic employment rose from 7,968,000 in 1966 to 8,851,000 in 1970—an average of 2.7 percent a year, as compared to the national average of all companies of only 1.8

51

percent. U.S. multinationals' overseas employment, however, rose over threefold from 1960 to 1972, from 458,000 to 1,411,034, obviously an economic benefit to the host countries and a·great achievement, too often overlooked.

1974 and After: The Third Epoch in the Modern History of the Multinationals

The curtain on this period was raised dramatically in October 1973. The Arab oil producers of the Persian Gulf, confronting the military power of Israel and the political and economic power of the booming West, were impelled in the one instance and encouraged in the other to exercise the prerogatives of a cartel and charge what the traffic would bear for their oil. Others are more critical of this development than I happen to be. There are powerful cartels in the West, and for years the leaders of these groups charged as much as they could for their products. One cannot but express some regret that the OPEC group adjusted the price so suddenly and to such a degree that it represented a serious threat to the rest of the world. Nevertheless, an accommodation is gradually developing, and I see no moral basis for criticism of these events.

The developing world learned a great deal from the action of the oil producers: similar cartels have since been organized by the countries producing copper and bauxite. This should result in better bargaining between producer and consumer and a fairer deal to the producing countries. I, for one, welcome these developments as an important step in bringing about a better distribution of income throughout the world.

Two other dramatic developments occurred at this time to mark the emergence of this third epoch. Both took place at the headquarters of the United Nations in May 1974. One was the adoption at a special session of the United Nations General Assembly of a "Declaration on the Establishment of a New Economic Order" and the promulgation of a "Charter of Economic Rights and Duties of States." This charter is a first attempt to formulate international rules to govern the relations between states and multinational companies.

The second development at the UN headquarters was a session at the Economic and Social Council devoted to "The Impact of Multinational Corporations on the Development Process and on International Relations."

These two events finally placed in focus the whole spectrum of multinational corporate activities and provided a blueprint to the developing world. A continuing and central effort is now joined to control the relations between states and multinational corporations.

These events have ushered in the third epoch of my brief history. We now have clear and specific guidelines for multinational company activities within the borders of a host country. These countries have the sovereign authority to enforce their requirements. All states, no matter how small, have powers to tax, set exchange controls, erect import and export controls, impose duties, appropriate, regulate, and nationalize—powers no company on earth possesses.

This should not imply, however, that the companies themselves have no responsibility for regulating their own conduct. Furthermore, continuing efforts to articulate more clearly and precisely the claims of both states and companies before international bodies will help to bring about more socially responsible corporate behavior.

Summary

During the first and second epochs in the modern chapter of this history there was justified criticism of the conduct of some of the multinationals in various developing countries. Companies such as IT&T and the copper producers in Chile can be properly singled out.

Lack of adequate social consciousness and an excessive obsession with the profit motive were prevalent.

Let us not, however, assign guilt by association. Even though there are offenders, all should not be condemned for the actions of few. In the long history of the multinational corporation this period was a brief one, and even then the rising expectations were served, certainly in part. More has been accomplished for the benefit of mankind by the engine of the profit motive than by appealing to the humanitarian feelings of either the East or the West.

Within only a few decades, the developing countries have been able to leap-frog across 2,000 years of history in terms of medical care, sanitation, educational infrastructure, agricultural improvements, communications and transportation—although they contributed little or nothing to the science that made these advances possible. Despite their histories, harsh climates, geography, and locations far from the industrial world, they have been linked to an international society. And this has been done by the private sector of our planetary society. ◉

2

FOREIGN AID

In the mid-1960s, when the following three NATO papers were presented, foreign aid still generally meant United States foreign aid. In 1964, for example, the United States alone contributed 58 percent of all the official development assistance (ODA) flowing from the developed to the underdeveloped nations, and no other country contributed more than 8 percent.

Within the United States, the ideological motive for giving foreign aid had become predominant. Aid was not only considered a Cold War weapon but it was generally given only in a way that benefitted and encouraged the free enterprise system. In 1964 the United States refused to finance a steel mill in India because the mill would have been controlled by the Indian government and would have competed with privately owned facilities. This short-sighted attitude — which fortunately no longer prevails — is criticized in the discussion of channels of aid in the first article in this section.

That 1964 paper also points out the need to eliminate crippling social customs, such as the caste system and discrimination based on race or sex.

In the same period, the Atlantic alliance was troubled by inflation, by French President Charles de Gaulle's go-it-alone philosophy, and most of all by the increasing U.S. involvement in the Vietnam War, to which most of the European nations were strongly opposed. Preoccupied with these cracks and strains, the alliance over-looked its obligations to provide aid to some of its own members, particularly Italy, Greece, and Turkey, as discussed in "Foreign Aid at Home," page 71.

A
BUSINESS VIEW OF
FOREIGN AID
(1964)

A discussion of the importance of directing for-eign aid toward ending superstitions, in order to bring the less-developed countries into the mod-ern world....The channels of foreign aid: all avail-able means, both private and governmental, should be employed.

Two aspects of foreign aid merit discussion at this time: first, the need to link foreign aid to human devel-opment, and second, the necessity of using all available economic facilities, governmental as well as private, to carry out development programs.

Social Development

Any approach to underdeveloped nations must first aim at enhancing the skills and capabilities of the peo-ple. Specific formulas for applying capital have their place but they often founder upon the conditions, moti-vations, and customs within individual societies.

In many areas, large numbers of people are not inte-grated into their country's national life. Society neither gains from their lives nor losses from their deaths; there is no social investment in them. It is like having a multi-tude of bank accounts with nothing on deposit. Long-term solutions must take this deprived part of our popu-lation into consideration. We must avoid programs that do not provide the seeds for continuation and growth.

Leaders of underdeveloped countries who are genu-inely concerned about their marginal populations often find it politically impossible or unpalatable to make the sweeping social changes that are necessary for foreign

Presented to the Economic Committee, North Atlantic Assembly. Paris, October 1964.

aid to be most efficiently absorbed. If we are to be innovative and realistic, we should consider linking to economic aid some formula requiring that a percentage of the amount advanced be matched by local funds earmarked for the development of human resources. There should be definite allocations to education (including administrative training), to health (including birth control information), and to welfare. Finally, some of the matching funds should go into educational programs aimed at eliminating customs and practices that are holding back social and economic progress. If this is argumentatively viewed as "interfering in internal affairs," so be it.

The earmarking of local currencies for such efforts would require national discipline, for the amounts must be generated internally. Nevertheless, if the underdeveloped countries genuinely wish Western society to help raise their living standards, they must be prepared to modify their social structures in order to make it possible to absorb the techniques and advantages they so urgently wish to have.

We should require aid recipients to accept conditions designed to bring about self-sufficiency in the future. Otherwise, we may alleviate the human suffering of the moment, but we will not fulfill a greater responsibility in these countries, which is to help build a national life that will endure.

Social change must accompany and reinforce economic change. India, for example, through laws passed in 1947 and 1955, took the first steps to abolish the caste system. Although it will require a generation or so to reach the goal, India is now moving in that direction. Along similar lines, we should try to persuade other countries to increase their efforts in education.

An outstanding example of a practice that hinders progress—one crying out for reform—can be found in societies where women are relegated to a minor role and are prevented from participating fully in national life. No country, as the United States has found, can afford such a waste of human resources. Women can make an enormous contribution in every professional field, law, business, teaching, medicine, and many other areas. In addition, women can develop and stimulate a progressive point of view because of their involvement with the upbringing of the new generation.

Improvements in social justice also are needed in developing countries to motivate their people to work purposefully and to realize that their own interest is served by breaking with age-old barriers.

Two U.S. studies demonstrate the direct relationship between human capital and economic growth. Edward F. Denison, in a paper for the Committee for Economic Development, attributes some 23 percent of the growth in real national income in the United States between 1929 and 1957 to the increased education of the labor force; another 20 percent is attributed to the advance of technological and managerial knowledge that permitted more to be produced from a given quantity of resources. Both of these values are greater than the contribution to growth made by the increase in physical capital, which accounted for only 15 percent of the total rise in real national income in the period. Another study, made by John W. Kendrick and published by Princeton University Press, estimates that human factors were responsible for almost half, or 1.6 percent per year, of the average productivity advance of 3.5 percent per year that prevailed in the United States over the long period 1889 to 1957.

Making the same point in an imaginative way, T. W. Schultz, a noted agricultural economist at the University of Chicago, has asked what would happen if India's population of 450 million, or an equivalent number from some other underdeveloped region, were miraculously exchanged for the population of the United States and Western Europe. Does anyone suppose that the gross national product of the Western countries for the succeeding year would rise, or even be maintained, with all their resources, industrial plant, and devices for capital formation?

If we do not put pressure on underdeveloped countries to cultivate their human resources and abandon voluntarily the traditional restraints of their national lives, in the end they will be rudely catapulted into the modern era by revolution or by ideologies that will force upon them an alien social structure—at the cost of human freedom. Foreign aid must be directed to the people, not just to the financial and political hierarchy. We seem often to have forgotten that the development of our industrial life has been keyed to an important extent to the labor movements. We must reckon with the needs of labor in our foreign initiatives.

Channels of Aid

What are the means of providing economic aid? One of the much debated questions in the West is whether foreign aid should be given chiefly or even exclusively through private entities in the developing countries or through government-controlled enterprises as well. This dispute tends to obscure the objectives. It is unlikely that the channels selected for foreign aid will be the paramount factor in determining the economic philosophy of a developing country.

We must carry on economic assistance through any and all existing conduits. The dearth of talent, organization, and technical know-how is so great, compared to national needs, that all available means ought to be used, public and private. Capital needs are so vast that there is ample room for both public and private enterprises to develop side-by-side under national disciplines consistent with free institutions.

There are many reasons why the role of government in underdeveloped economies is far greater than in the more industrially mature societies of the West. Other parts of the world cannot be expected to develop in a free enterprise system identical to that of the West.

The long history and flexibility of European society should permit it to take a broad view of the role of the state in the economy. In many European countries, including France, West Germany, the United Kingdom, and Italy, the state owns air and rail transportation, TV and radio, telephone, and telegraph facilities. French Premier Georges Pompidou pointed out that France has evolved her own economic pattern "half way between the socialist systems and those that are capitalistic in the strict sense of the word." The French state is the country's largest producer of automobiles, and it also controls the coal mines, the production and distribution of gas and electricity, the railroads, a large portion of air and sea transport, the majority of the insurance companies and banks, and the greater part of aircraft construction. Yet, France is basically a private-property, free-enterprise society. As Pompidou has said, in the final analysis France realizes [and may still, even in 1978's period of Eurocommunism] that her economic advance and well-being depend upon the spirit of enterprise and initiative among private business leaders.

In Italy, to cite another example, the government owns or controls substantial manufacturing, service, and mining enterprises including iron and steel facilities, the Alfa-Romeo automobile concern, firms producing motorcycles, railway equipment, ships, electromechanical products, chemicals, petrochemicals (plastics) and synthetic rubber, oil, and natural gas. Nevertheless, these government-owned or controlled enterprises must, in most instances, compete with privately owned firms that are engaged in the same or similar activities.

To assure permanent economic growth in the underdeveloped countries, the seeds of domestic capital formation must be nurtured. The Western world has not yet been able to devise a mechanism for exporting its savings, on the scale required to develop other countries, without upsetting its own balance of payments. As incomes rise in the countries receiving aid, internal saving mechanisms must be organized and their use encouraged. According to United Nations figures, the ratio of net domestic saving to gross domestic product is about 10 percent for the developed countries, but only a small fraction of that in most underdeveloped areas. During the decade of the 1950s the savings ratio actually declined in about half the underdeveloped countries.

Of course, the countries receiving aid today find it infinitely more difficult to initiate a savings pattern than did the Western countries in the period following the industrial revolution. Nevertheless, there are some directions in which it is possible to work.

To cite one example, a fundamental tool in the accumulation of savings is life insurance. It not only preserves and strengthens the human fabric of society but also creates a pool of funds which can be used for investment. Ways of spreading the risk on an international scale must be sought so that rates are not prohibitive for low income populations. Here is a real opportunity for imaginative private enterprise. Spreading the risk more widely on an international scale, with government help if necessary, would enable the more highly developed countries to subsidize the rates for the less developed. This would scarcely be more of a burden than the direct taxes that now provide funds for foreign aid projects of less durable value.

To encourage private enterprise, Germany in 1963 granted special tax concessions on investments in underdeveloped areas to stimulate international activities by German corporations and investors. Some such incentives exist in the United States, but much more could be done. Internationally oriented corporations provide a highly useful vehicle for carrying out foreign aid in the tradition of Western society.

Our own economies have been evolving for nearly two hundred years, so we must be tolerant if it takes other countries some time to attain elements of our type of society. But the present underdeveloped countries cannot wait two hundred years. It may be necessary for them to evolve a somewhat different economic and social structure in order to achieve their goals more quickly. It is a sobering thought that although the advance of science and technology has been miraculous, and billions of dollars have been spent applying our knowledge to the raising of living standards, there are more people in the world who live in poverty today than there were fifty years ago.

By the year 2000 the population of the underdeveloped nations will constitute an even higher percentage of world population than today. Can these countries ever take their place beside us as economically mature and independent societies in which all people enjoy a reasonable degree of security, dignity and opportunity? It is a challenge that defies all but the bravest and boldest imaginations. By assigning a higher priority to the development of human resources, and using every available channel for aid, the challenge can be met. ◉

Postscript

In the 1970s, which the U.N. calls the "Development Decade," a greater proportion of aid is being given for people programs, for food and poverty programs, and to solve some of the social problems of development mentioned in this paper.

Another encouraging sign is the increase in the savings ratios of the LDCs, which stood at 21.8 percent in 1975. Much of this increase, however, is accounted for by the oil producing states of OPEC, which achieved a 37.7 percent savings ratio, and by foreign investment, which helped raise the savings ratio of the nonpetroleum LDCs to 15.5 percent in 1975.

FOREIGN AID NEEDS AN EDUCATION
(1965)

A call for more foreign aid to be directed toward education and technical aid as the best means to achieve economic growth.

Within the past several years many governments, international agencies, and private charitable institutions have stepped up aid and technical assistance to educational programs all over the undeveloped world. Universities have been built, training colleges for teachers have been opened, and research programs in education have been started. All forms of aid have been provided, from computers for scientific research to textbooks and pencils for primary schools. Although this has been encouraging, it is not enough.

It is not enough because literally hundreds of problems still call out for a solution. For example, a task force of the Organization of American States estimated that between 50 percent and 60 percent of all Latin American expenditures on education is wasted, much of it through literacy that is lost shortly after it is gained. Other significant problems include the relationship between education needs and future manpower requirements, and the ratio of secondary schools to primary schools. Furthermore, research has not yet determined the relationship between the retention of literacy and the age when teaching begins. Relatively small expenditures in such areas could improve the effectiveness of existing foreign educational aid and of locally sponsored educational projects.

A much greater emphasis should be placed on education specifically tailored to meet the economic environment of the people involved. It has been said that

Presented to the Economic Committee, NATO Parliamentarians' Conference. New York, October 1965.

increased education is responsible for excessive migrations from the farms to towns. If this is so, it is not education but miseducation. Surely, increased literacy and simple technological know-how in rural areas of developing countries can be translated into higher agricultural production, thus providing the economic incentive and sense of self-fulfillment that will make migration less appealing. If rural education results in people turning their backs on the immediate advantages of their home environment and propelling themselves into the squalid and precarious life of the city slums then one can only conclude that they have been taught the wrong things.

There are at least two specific ways in which educational aid can be increased in breadth and effectiveness. First, the mature countries of the world should participate actively in long-term educational planning in cooperation with the recipient countries. Long-term planning is particularly vital to the success of an industrial system. To be most effective, it must be projected for some twenty years into the future, for obviously, if planning is to work, the recipient country must know what it can and cannot reasonably expect.

Second, the more-developed countries must be prepared to provide more than the basic capital for education; they must also provide the day-to-day operating costs of the educational apparatus. Most aid to education today is given to cover construction costs, or in special crash programs for technical assistance. Presumably this is done on the theory that the recipient has the funds to pay for operating expenditures, which is simply not true. Actually, in most underdeveloped countries the public sector's contribution to the GNP is seldom above 10 percent of the total. Of this, it is invariably true that all too little can be spared for critically needed education expenditures. (In the industrialized countries, the public sector contributes 16 percent to 19 percent of GNP.)

Economic aid to developing nations has not worked

out nearly as well as we once hoped it would. When the mature countries launched full-scale aid to the emerging nations, they did so with much the same motives that lay behind the Marshall Plan. They have not, however, had anything like the same success. Most underdeveloped countries were unable to put the aid to maximum use. They lacked full comprehension of its value, and they did not have the human resources and technical abilities to apply it properly.

And yet, while it is common enough to hear lamentations on this state of affairs, attempts to grapple with and solve the problem have been inadequate when compared to the magnitude of the issue. More effort, time and money must be devoted to improve and encourage the growth of human resources and technical abilities of younger countries. Aid to education should be stepped up—at the expense of conventional economic aid if necessary.

Despite a growing literature on the subject, we have not yet fully understood how deeply a country's economic development relies on social factors. On the surface, these human factors seem to have only an indirect relationship to the actual machinery of production. The little knowledge we possess on this matter, however, indicates that economic growth is built, first and foremost, on human resources. Mines, coffee plantations, textile factories—these do not by themselves create a viable social and political life for a country. The human beings involved must be integrated into a social and political framework to generate the development impetus from below.

The process of development is not exclusively social or technical or economic or political, but a blend of all these forces which must be used in combination to bring about development and change. Education is the catalyst. The latent desire to move out of the backwaters of near primitive societies into the modern world exists in almost every developing country. It is our task to nurture that impulse.

It is a severe indictment of our foreign aid program that after so many years of effort, and so many billions of dollars spent, we still are not stimulating the internal energies of underdeveloped countries on the scale necessary for adequate, self-sustained growth. In 1964, the Society for International Development estimated that only 12½ percent of the potential human resources in emerging nations was being used. Of course, education is not a panacea, and increased education—as many are aware from bringing up their own children—does not always guarantee significantly improved results. Nevertheless, although prudence cautions against making exaggerated claims for the benefits of education, the fact is that without it, no development is possible. This is supported by studies at the University of Chicago, which suggest that an adult literacy rate of at least 40 percent is a primary requirement for development. What chance of economic development, then, do most African countries have, when only about 25 percent of the children between the age of six and fourteen years attend school?

It is in the interest of the more developed countries of the world to sponsor cultural integration between themselves and the developing countries. For political and humanitarian reasons, the increasing gulf between the rich and the poor must be closed. Moreover, rising trade and technological progress have made clear the need for commonly understood terms of reference. We, the economically advanced nations, possess the knowledge and the power, and it is our responsibility to spread this knowledge widely and thoroughly.

It is not that we seek a homogeneous and bland "international culture." We know that the customs and values, the technology and procedures, that we have developed over the last few hundred years will naturally have to undergo modification before the developing nations adopt them. These modifications, however, when harnessed to the indigenous evolutionary processes of the developing countries, will surely produce a viable and better society.

The need for increased aid to education on all fronts is clear-cut and urgent. I am not suggesting that it is a cure for all the acute problems confronting the under-developed world. But it is a vital ingredient, and an absolute prerequisite for economic growth. It should be recognized as such. ◉

FOREIGN
AID AT HOME
(1967)

A recommendation that the more economically advanced members of NATO should give more aid to its less developed members, to preserve the strength of the West.

For the past twenty years the plight of the underdeveloped countries has been one of the central preoccupations in international affairs. Without underestimating the importance of this subject, the time has come to look in the opposite direction—towards the problems of the more developed world. It is useful to take stock of the strength and weaknesses of the Western nations, not only from motives of self-interest, but also because ultimately the peace and prosperity of much of the world depends on the vitality of the West and on the capacity of the West to make strong and intelligent responses to a multitude of global issues.

So the question may be posed: How strong is the West, and how strong are the members of NATO? This difficult question does not admit easy answers. But some of the available evidence suggests that there are cracks and fissures that could have grave consequences in the future. Moreover, these weaknesses appear at a time when it is obvious that the challenges in the years ahead will be more frequent and larger than at any time in the past.

A catalog of the present difficulties of most Western nations would certainly be longer than five years ago, perhaps longer than ten years ago. Some of the old political solidarity among Western nations has vanished, particularly in the field of foreign policy. Economically, it often seems as if we have reached an apogee in the

Presented to the Political Committee, North Atlantic Assembly. Brussels, October 1967.

West. The exuberance of postwar economic rebuilding has gone.

There are signs of serious malfunctions in the productive apparatus of several Western nations that only a few years ago seemed capable of an endless series of economic triumphs. On top of this we have recurring worries over the technological gap and financial squabbles over who should bear certain costs for our mutual defense. Furthermore, there are conspicuous inequities in the standards of living of NATO members—discrepancies that have not so far received the attention they deserve. Heretofore we have not sought to tackle these and other mutual problems on a systematic basis. The general assumption appears to have been that these headaches would be solved in good time. This muddling-through approach is no longer adequate. We cannot afford to be casual.

Other regional, ethnic, and cultural groupings among the nations of the globe are emerging and becoming stronger. What is more, population in many of these areas is growing at a far quicker rate than in the West. Overpopulation in these nations inevitably creates domestic pressures which lead to aggressive and expansionist policies.

In spite of the difficulties within the NATO countries, there is much in which we can take pride. It is worth noting that over the past one hundred years most of the nations that today comprise NATO warred with one another intermittently. Yet currently there exists a sympathy between them that would have been unthinkable a century ago, or even twenty years ago.

This is no small achievement. Slowly but surely—sometimes willingly, sometimes under duress—these nations have come to share more and more common ground. There is naturally a wide diversity among them. What is remarkable, however, is the extent to which they share humanistic values, political institutions, aptitudes, and beliefs about the nature of man and society.

It must be admitted that the unity of the Western alliance is not entirely of its own making. The external pressure of the Cold War played a decisive role. But we must not let détente or the thaw in the Cold War create an atmosphere in which there is less unity and cooperation. The solidarity of the West—if it is not to decline—must be nurtured and fostered from within; it must be reinvigorated by our conscious decisions to secure our interests and maintain our vitality.

In 1918, Oswald Spengler, the German historian, published his famous work, *The Decline of the West*, which prophesied an imminent decline for most of the current members of NATO. His prophecy remains unfulfilled. However, greater threats to the West can be expected in the future.

According to the United Nations Department of Economic and Social Affairs, world population in 1960 stood at 3 billion and will reach 6 billion by the year 2000.

It is significant that out of the estimated net increase of 3 billion, the countries of the North American continent and Europe, including the Soviet Union, will have a net gain of merely half a billion. By the year 2000 the technologically advanced nations of the northern half of the globe will have around 22 percent of the total world population, compared to more than 28 percent in 1960.

The West, therefore, faces a sharp reduction in its population representation. National population is itself a factor in power politics—as we repeatedly admit when thinking about China. It should be remembered that power is not entirely relative. It is, for example, not difficult to conceive of several large, presently underdeveloped countries becoming major powers with only a very small increment in their economic output and technological abilities.

For the past fifteen years the nations of the West have spent much of their patrimony on aid to the underdeveloped world. This was necessary and appropriate, and it should not be discontinued. But at the same time, except for military defense, the nations of the West have neglected to pursue some of their long-range interests closer to home. For instance, they have neglected to strengthen and assist the weaker members within the Western alliance. The following data sheds some light on this issue.

United States foreign aid to Western Europe declined from $4.3 billion in 1949 to $58 million in 1965. Meanwhile, between 1956 and 1965, net official grants to the underdeveloped world by NATO countries increased from $3.1 billion to $5.9 billion [and to $13.6 billion in 1976]. It goes without saying that these figures largely reflect Marshall Plan spending, the subsequent European economic growth, and the succeeding ability of the European nations to undertake assistance to the less developed countries.

Should we not expend more energy and attention within the shores and borders of the Western alliance? The West could be and must be stronger. Even in the area of economic development there are regions within countries, and in some cases entire nations, that need all the skills and resources we can muster.

In other words, I suggest we examine our priorities very carefully and seriously question the whole intellectual system on which we conceive our self-interest. If it appears that the case for increased mutual aid among Western nations is a good one, then NATO could become increasingly useful to us all. NATO, as we all know, was created as a specific response to a foreboding set of circumstances. The conditions have changed, yet NATO remains a well-tuned instrument that can be put to more ambitious nonmilitary purposes.

NATO has actually already taken a few tentative steps in this direction. Aid has been offered to some of the less fortunate NATO members. But the potential for this kind of activity has only barely been tapped. Furthermore, when the NATO treaty comes to be rewritten in 1969, we should place at its heart a statement of objectives that will stimulate cooperation and mutual assistance between members at all levels and in all relevant areas.

We all share an obligation to maintain and increase the strength of the West, and each of us has a grave responsibility for the other's welfare. The nations of the West created the modern world. It would be lamentable if the verdict of history was that we failed to do everything in our power to protect and preserve it.◉

Postscript

Italy's continuing crises in 1978 underline the extent of NATO's neglect of its weaker members. Considering the historical and cultural role that Italy has occupied in the development of Western civilization and the geopolitics of today, it is inexcusable that we have not included this country, with its poverty-stricken southern parts, in some significant support program.

3

OIL
AND THE COST
OF ENERGY

Oil and energy problems are such a great part of our economic lives today that it is difficult to recall how little attention was paid to the politico-economic situation in the Middle East before the OPEC oil embargo of 1973.

The first of the papers on this subject, "NATO's Second Front," was written in 1968, when Europe was the prime concern of political leaders on both sides of the Atlantic and when most of the world blithely assumed that cheap petroleum would continue gushing out of the Middle East forever. If some of the suggestions in this paper had been heeded at the time, many of our later crises and emergencies might have been avoided.

The second paper, "Moslem Oil and the Yankee Dollar," was presented in September 1973, and within a few weeks the Yom Kippur War and the Arab oil embargo turned the potential dangers it described into a very real crisis. Four years later the U.S. government is finally beginning to recognize the need for a comprehensive energy policy such as the one outlined in this paper, but even President Carter's much-discussed energy program is too feeble to do the job required.

77

In February 1974, during the panicky winter of fuel shortages and filling station lines, the third paper in this section, a speech at the University of Pennsylvania, assessed the long-range implications of the crisis and made clear that the price of oil, not the supply, would be the real problem for the next decade also.

NATO'S SECOND FRONT: BACKGROUND TO THE OIL CRISIS
(1968)

A warning that NATO has ignored the Middle East, in which it has a vital and most serious stake....Outlines Soviet military and economic influence in that area....Discusses the importance of oil to the region....Points out the area's need for development, which NATO should respond to more actively to ameliorate the poverty of the region and thus reduce dangerous tensions.

NATO's European front against the Communist bloc has been its strongest feature—defended in depth, dependable and resolute.

NATO's second front, in the Middle East, has been neglected. Our response to the Soviet's drive into this area has been totally inadequate. The failure to protect Western economic and diplomatic interests has slowly impaired our capacity to bring peace to this turbulent region.

While NATO and the Warsaw Pact countries were concentrating primarily on European antagonisms, Russia itself continued to strengthen its position in the Middle East. It was able to capitalize successfully on the end of the colonial epoch in that area. The Soviet presence there today creates a second economic, diplomatic, and military front for the West.

The Middle East is an area of such natural concern for NATO that it is difficult to understand its neglect. Italy, Turkey, and Greece, three NATO members, are surrounded by mountains and their trade routes are limited to the air and sea, thus making the freedom of the Mediterranean a necessity for survival. Air distances

Presented to the Political and Military Committees, North Atlantic Assembly. Paris, October 1968.

are modest: Cairo is 765 miles from Algiers; and Athens, 750 miles from Tel Aviv. Given this exposure, NATO's effectiveness would be impaired should its southern flank members be unable to meet their commitments. And, of course, these three nations could themselves each be drawn into any Middle East conflict.

Even those NATO countries that are physically distant from the Middle East have a great common stake in the region, for without Middle Eastern oil the strength of European and North American economies would be severely impaired. NATO, therefore, must do all in its power to help establish stability and tranquility in the region and, most certainly, to balance the continually growing Russian military and diplomatic offensive. If we do not, then the Soviet dangers that NATO has successfully blocked on the eastern borders of West Germany may only have been submerged, to reappear as a reality in the Middle East.

We should remember that Russia has a long history of territorial ambition in this part of the world. Ninety years ago the Tsars coveted Turkey and Iran, and before that, Turkey fought Russia over what was then known as Bessarabia. After World War II, the Russians made another bid for these two countries but were rebuffed when CENTO was created as a countermeasure. Recently, the Soviets have scored a greater success in Syria, Iraq, Egypt, Algeria, and in Aden—a success that coincides with the decline of British and French influence in the region. We may not be able to determine precisely what the aims of Soviet Middle Eastern policy are. But there is considerable evidence to suggest that those goals are substantial, that they represent a grave danger to the West, that they involve major commitments of capital and prestige—and that the Soviets are embarked on a long-term effort.

Soviet presence in the Middle East has taken many forms. It is widely believed, for instance, that the Russians played an influential diplomatic role in abetting Arab anti-Israeli and anti-Western policies in the first half of 1967. For example, after the Six Day War the Soviet Union dramatically increased its influence, by quickly refurbishing and modernizing the defeated armies of the Arabs—with surface-to-air naval missiles. [Nevertheless, in the two years following, Egypt's President Anwar Sadat dramatically and pragmatically broke with the Soviets.]

The Soviet Navy first began to cruise the Mediterranean in about 1964. Previously it had confined itself to the Caspian, the Black Sea, and the Vladivostock area. The Soviet Mediterranean naval contingent has grown to the point where in 1968 it numbers between 40 and 50 ships, some of which are missile armed cruisers. The U.S. Sixth Fleet, one of the most formidable armadas afloat in the world, deploys about 50 ships in the Mediterranean, with an estimated striking power that is greater than the Russians'. Yet, if the Russian Mediterranean naval build-up continues, NATO's sea power in the region will be seriously challenged.

Russia has constructed its first helicopter aircraft carrier and more are on the way. The Middle East would appear to be one of the most likely places for these craft to be deployed. Fortunately, NATO has not been entirely idle in the face of this threat, but NATO should be considerably more active in this regard.

Soviet trade in the Middle East is also in the ascendancy. The United Arab Republic's exports to the Communist world rose from $244 million in 1960 to $316 million in 1966—a 30 percent jump that accounted for all of the U.A.R.'s increase in external trade. [In 1975, Egyptian exports to the Eastern bloc totalled $931 million, or 68 percent of all exports.] Syria's trade with the bloc actually tripled from 1960 to 1966. Because of the underdeveloped state of these economies, the trade figures do not loom large in the Soviet Union total, but they weave a web about the Arab nations—as do the aid, technical assistance, and the shipments of wheat.

The latest evidence of Soviet expansion in the Middle East concerns oil. The Russians have agreed to explore for oil in Iraq, Iran, and Egypt, and they have bid for oil ventures in Algeria, Syria, and Kuwait. They have a strong economic justification for these efforts. The Soviet Union is the fifth largest oil producer in the world, a large exporter to Communist bloc countries and to Western Europe as well. In 1967, it produced 2.1 billion barrels of oil and exported 366.5 million barrels. Evidence is accumulating that by the 1970s Russia will need oil to supplement its exports. Thus, like Western nations, it has a motive in looking for alternative sources of supply. But one must also assume a diplomatic and political intent to unsettle traditional relations in oil production and marketing, and to interfere with the West's supply of this vital fuel.

All of us know of Egypt's Aswan Dam, financed with 1 billion dollars of Soviet aid. To this has been added another spectacular showcase project. In May 1968, the U.A.R. and the Soviet Union announced that the latter would build an $800 million iron and steel complex at Helvan, fifteen miles south of Cairo. This project will provide employment for 12,000 workers and is intended to make the U.A.R. self-sufficient in steel. Similarly, in return for long-term supplies of natural gas, the Soviets will build a $500 million steel plant in Iran.

We have not yet matched this Soviet challenge with sufficient thrust or imagination. NATO's reaction in the Middle East has been slow and, for the most part, sluggish. As a force for peace and prosperity in this area NATO has been woefully inadequate.Obviously the situation does not call for a military solution. What is needed is a common and determined NATO policy combining flexible approaches on the economic, diplomatic, and military fronts. We must accept some measure of Soviet presence, but we must not, and need not, allow the Russians an excessive influence on the course of events.We can limit Soviet influence by taking a greater and more activist role ourselves.

I have spoken of NATO's second front. But it is not a front in the conventional use of the word. It has no set frontiers, no need of great standing armies. The enemy is not only the growing power and influence of the Soviet Union in the area, but poverty, malnutrition, and ignorance among the people themselves. We should give the most careful thought to the realities of our southeastern flank. ◉

MOSLEM OIL
AND THE YANKEE
DOLLAR
(1973)

A major paper, written just before the Arab oil embargo, calling attention to the growing economic power of the Moslem countries and predicting a new Islamic Renaissance....Some history of Islam....Statistics underlying the world's dependence on Arab oil....Points out the possibility of production restrictions and the danger of a blockade of constricted tanker lanes....Discusses the windfall profits of Moslem oil, and predicts that oil prices will increase....Suggests that surplus Arab profits may be invested in the West and may also help the economic growth of the less developed countries....Concluding with a call for a common energy policy to conserve oil and develop alternative sources of energy.

It is a curious fact that the cradle of civilization—the great land bridge connecting Asia to Africa—after being bypassed for some fifteen hundred years has become again the focus of great importance and world attention. The eastern shore of this land bridge, with its oil resources, is now providing much of the material sinews of life to the West—as it once provided the world with three great religions and much more moral and spiritual fiber.

The present output of oil from the countries on the western shore (Iraq, Kuwait, Saudi Arabia, Qatar, Abu Dhabi, and the small sheikdoms of the Trucial Coast), along with Iran on the eastern side of the Persian Gulf, approaches 21 million barrels per day. This is greater than the current daily consumption of the United States (16 million barrels) and greater than the combined con-

Presented to the North Atlantic Assembly, Ankara, September 1973.

sumption of Western Europe and Japan (19 million barrels daily). Furthermore, construction is already under way to increase Saudi Arabian production to 14 million barrels per day from its current level of 9 million barrels. The new level of output from this small country alone, which has a population of 7 million, would be about 25 percent greater than the present U.S. production. It is believed that Saudi Arabian reserves could support an output of 20 million barrels per day.

The oil capital of the world is shifting from Houston, Texas, to Dhahran, Saudi Arabia, as a result of the Middle East oil boom and the powerful financial implications of the huge oil revenues that will be generated there.

An Oil-Financed Islamic Renaissance

This new-found wealth hopefully will bring about a rebirth of the Golden Age of the Arab world that burst forth some fifteen hundred years ago from the burnt sands of the Arabian desert. History records the remarkable ascendancy of Islam that took place within 200 years of the founding of the Moslem faith by the Prophet Mohammed at Medina in 622. It reached eastward through Persia and India, onward to Malaysia and Indonesia, and westward across North Africa to Spain.

The genius of Islam flowered into matchless artistic, intellectual, and political achievements. Since Mohammed wished his followers to study the Koran, learning was from the beginning highly valued. Moslem scholars collected the learning of the ancient Greek and Roman world, and added to and expanded it with their own contributions. Ptolemy was rediscovered. The Arabs made a map of the world in the tenth century, an achievement which might rank with photographs of the moon today. At a time when everyone in Europe believed the world to be flat, an Arabian named Al-Ma'mun estimated, in 830, the circumference of the world at 24,000 miles and the diameter at 6,500 miles.

By studying the writings of the Hindus, the Moslems developed their own systems of mathematics. Working in the first half of the ninth century, Al-Khwarismi adapted the Hindu invention of the zero and devised our numeral system which to this day is called "Arabic." In yet another field, the surgeon Abu-al-Quasim compiled a book of medicine which was the standard text in Europe for centuries. So rich was Moslem learning, in fact, that it became the inspiration for what we now call the European Renaissance. Urban life flourished. In the thirteenth century, Baghdad had a population of over 1 million until it was decimated by the Mongols in 1258; Paris then had a population of only 250,000, and New York City may not even have been settled by the Indians.

Islam is a missionary religion, and in recent years it has been making inroads into Black Africa. Nigeria is an outstanding example and in some sub-Saharan states Christianity is now regarded as an expression of imperialism. Most Moslem countries are poor: few are blessed with oil or can expect the riches that oil will bring.

Although there are many Moslem countries that will earn no oil income, there have been plans for sharing the wealth since the first Arab Oil Congress in Cairo in 1959, when the Lebanese delegation proposed a sharing of oil royalties for development purposes. To date, no overall wealth-sharing plan exists, but the Kuwaitis, to their credit, have provided over $350 million in development loans through the Kuwait Fund for Arab Economic Development (KFAED); plans are now in the making for a much broader-based loan agency and fund.

King Faisal of Saudi Arabia, who takes seriously his role as spiritual leader of Islam, has directed loans to Moslem non-Arab states as well as, of course, to Arab nations. As *the Economist* has noted, "Recent [Saudi Arabian] help to Somalia, Niger, Uganda, and Oman has moved beyond the previous gifts for mosque buildings and in some instances it has attracted the attention of the World Bank, which has offered technical assistance to complement it." Again in his spiritual role, King Faisal sponsors the annual Islamic pilgrimage to Mecca which brings some 2,500,000 Moslems to that religious shrine.

Today, the priceless Moslem heritage that we have described stands waiting to be renewed. It could change the economic, political, and even social patterns of the world as we know it.

Oil Production and Consumption

The dominant position of oil in world energy use has come about for a variety of reasons, but essentially because of its easy access, abundance, and low price.To some extent this has had adverse implications insofar as it has stimulated an often profligate and unjustifiable use of oil. In addition, the development of other sources of energy and fuel has been neglected because petroleum, until recently, cost so little.

Energy consumption in the non-Communist world is growing at an annual rate of nearly 6 percent; should this rate continue, oil consumption will reach 71 million barrels per day in 1980. [Rising prices and conservation have sharply cut the growth in oil consumtpion. Between 1972 and 1976, U.S. consumption increased from 16 to 17 million barrels per day, while other non-Communist countries' consumption held steady. It is now estimated that the non-Communist world will consume only about 56 million barrels per day in 1980—compared to 40 million in 1970 and 45 million in 1976—but will reach the 71 million barrel level of consumption in 1985.]

Until recently, the United States provided for its accelerated growth in energy consumption with only relatively modest imports because of its own domestic oil, gas, and coal production. Current American oil imports, approximately 5 million barrels per day, or 30 percent of our oil needs, come mainly from Canada and

Venezuela, but from now on the increasing requirements of the United States will have to be met by rapidly rising imports from the Moslem countries.[By 1976,
because of a decline in domestic production, the United
States was already importing 8.9 million barrels of oil
per day, more than half its petroleum needs. This
import requirement is expected to remain about the
same through 1980 even if domestic production rises
again.]

The oil strike in Alaska, which has been given such
publicity, must be seen in its proper perspective. It is
hoped the Alaskan pipeline will accommodate 1 million
barrels per day when completed in 1977 [actual 1977
flow: 800,000 barrels per day], and this could conceiv-
ably be doubled by 1980, at which time this source
would provide some eight to nine percent of U.S. petroleum needs. However, this estimated 1980 production
would equal less than 2.5 percent of world needs at that
time, and therefore would ease world supply problems
only slightly.

From another point of view, Alaska's Prudhoe Bay oil
discovery is estimated to contain 10 billion barrels. The
entire North Slope might contain 30 billion barrels but
no responsible source will currently substantiate the
latter figure. In any event, the 10 billion barrels figure
will be only 1¼ times U.S. estimated requirements for a
single year by 1980. The 30 billion barrel figure would
take care of less than four years' consumption at that
time.

Western Europe and Japan are almost totally dependent on Moslem oil. Fortunately, there is a substantial
supply of oil developing in the North Sea, the full extent
of which is not yet known. Japan, however, rapidly
emerging as the second largest industrial power in the
world, has no indigenous fossil fuel resources.

In any event, there seems to be no danger of a world-
wide physical shortage of oil over the next fifteen years.
Current non-Communist world consumption is on the
order of 16 billion barrels a year, with a projected need

for 25 billion barrels [now estimated at 20.5 billion] by 1980. Proven oil reserves are estimated at more than 500 billion barrels, of which approximately 300 billion barrels are in the Middle East and concentrated around the Persian Gulf. This would indicate a reserve of only twenty years, based on 1980 projected requirements. It is probable, however, that these reserve figures are understated. Saudi Arabia, for instance, is thought to have as much as two to four times its "published proved" reserves of 145 billion barrels. In addition, higher prices and further technological advances should, of course, increase these estimates. Moreover, potential large-scale access to other sources, such as the oil shale deposits in the United States and the Athabasca tar sands in Canada, are not included in these calculations. In any event, for such an essential element of survival, hypothetical assumptions and conjectures cannot be relied upon. The intermediate and long-term reserve position is in a critical phase.

Although, as stated, there is no immediate danger of an inadequate supply of oil, there is the reality of production restrictions, and the ever-present hazard of a Middle Eastern conflict. By a quirk of providence, the oil-rich countries of the Middle East have few other resources, and, knowing this, they will prudently husband their oil against the time when it will be exhausted. Kuwait has already restricted its production to three million barrels per day, and Libya has likewise restricted its production to 2.2 million barrels per day. Present plans call for Saudi Arabian production to rise from 9 million to 14 million barrels per day by 1977 and, further, to 20 million at a later date. This last figure never may be reached, and production may level off at some point in the 1973—1977 range. [It did, at 9.1 million.] Such possible restrictions, however, are highly conjectural, depending on whether Saudi Arabia and other rich producers decide to keep their oil in the ground, or convert it into another form of capital above ground.

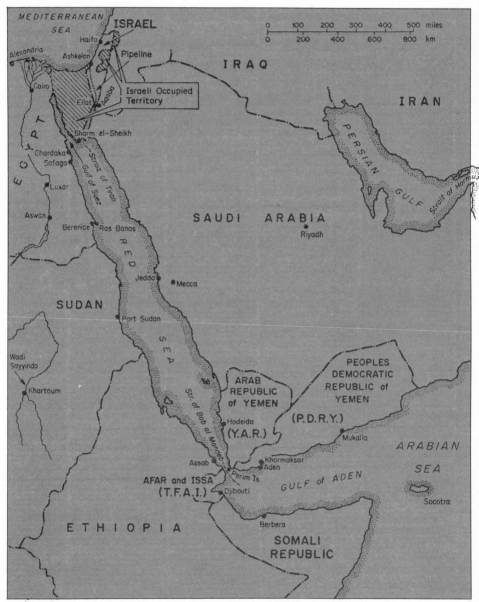

G. Hartfield Ltd.

THE RED SEA AND THE PERSIAN GULF

The point to bear in mind is that a very serious situation could easily arise if one or more Middle Eastern producers restricts production, or if an oil cut-off occurs as the result of political or military factors [as it did in the oil embargo of 1973].

Security of the Tanker Lanes

A fascinating feature of the world's dependence on shipments of Middle East oil concerns geography and the oil traffic that moves through two relatively little-known and narrow straits, the Strait of Hormuz and the Strait of Bab-el-Mandeb.

The Strait of Hormuz is located at the foot of the Persian Gulf. Approximately 26 miles wide, it connects the Persian Gulf with the Gulf of Oman and the Arabian Sea and thus provides access to the Indian Ocean and the Pacific. The Strait is formed by a peninsula that thrusts out toward Iran from the Trucial States on the lower eastern end of the Arabian Peninsula. The strait threads its way around this bulge. Three small islands within the Strait were taken over by Iran recently to safeguard its own national interest.

Through this passageway there move more than 17 million barrels of oil daily, or approximately 90 percent of the oil produced in Iran, Iraq, Kuwait, Saudi Arabia, Qatar, Abu Dhabi, and other less important producing areas.

The second vital gateway is the Strait of Bab-el-Mandeb, the southern entrance to the Red Sea. All transport into the Red Sea from the Gulf of Aden, the Arabian Sea, and the Indian Ocean must navigate this waterway, which is bordered on the Arabian side by Yemen and the Democratic Republic of Yemen, and on the African side by French Somaliland and Ethiopia's province of Eritrea, with the Somali Democratic Republic nearby. [In 1978, French Somaliland is independent Djibouti; Somali is at war with Ethiopia, and the Soviet Union is heavily involved on the Ethiopian side.] These are all countries with volatile histories, all obviously subject to power pressures of various sorts. The Strait itself is divided by Perim Island into two straits, the larger one, on the African side, being nine miles wide and quite deep; the one on the Arab side is a mile and a half wide and more shallow.

Through this Strait moves the oil that is headed for the Gulf of Aqaba and the Trans-Israel Pipeline terminus at Elath, which is being expanded to carry approximately 600,000 barrels a day across Israel to Mediterranean ports. The significance of Bab-el-Mandeb will increase dramatically when the SUMED (Suez-Mediterranean) pipeline parallel to the Suez Canal is opened. SUMED will be suppled by Middle East oil via this Strait and the Red Sea (see below).

The political stability of the area around the Strait has been in doubt since England pulled out east of Suez and the Russian naval presence increased. History may be written here again, as it was at the turn of the sixteenth century when Portugal established a great blockade outside the Strait. The blockade stifled profitable two-way Venetian and other Mediterranean trade that moved by trans-shipment across Egypt and through the Strait.

Oil Prices

Jahangir Amuzegar, the Iranian Ambassador-at-Large in charge of the Iranian Economic Mission in Washington [now Iran's foreign minister], in a *Foreign Affairs* article in July 1973, pointed out that extraction costs in the Middle East are only a fraction of what they are elsewhere in the world: only 10 cents a barrel on the average, as compared to roughly 51 cents in Venezuela, 82 cents in Indonesia, and $1.31 in the United States. "Since oil of the same quality is bound to obtain uniform f.o.b. prices in the world free markets," Amuzegar wrote, "Middle Eastern and North African crudes have up to now offered their owners an enormous windfall

profit—what economists call Ricardian rent—
stemming from the difference in production costs compared with Mexican Gulf suppliers and other high-cost
producers."

Ambassador Amuzegar asserts that "the postwar history of the oil industry is a story of a continued jockey-
ing among petroleum exporters and the oil majors to
divide (and appropriate) this rent." He credits OPEC
with the turnabout that now assures the oil producers
the major share. "In any event," he goes on, "the price of
crude oil will be subject primarily to the primitive laws
of supply and demand. The probabilities are that its
price will continue in an uptrend until competing sources of energy and alternative sources of crude are developed in large enough quantities to hold down the price."

As long as oil prices were artificially low, oil consumption grew far out of proportion to what would
have been normal. High prices will now stimulate the
production of competing sources of energy and at the
same time discourage the profligate use of oil. Furthermore, the taxes which the governments of the consuming countries levied on the use of petroleum products
were practical only because the products were sold at a
level that permitted them to bear this tax burden. The
real cost of this dismal chain of events must now be met
in terms of necessary but expensive crash programs for
the development of alternative energy resources.

Financial Repercussions

What are the financial implications of the massive
accumulation of foreign exchange by the OPEC members? By the end of this decade, oil income of the OPEC
countries is expected to exceed $63 billion *annually.* The
cost to the United States will be in excess of $25 billion a
year, and for Western Europe and Japan about $36 bil-
lion and $24 billion a year. Moreover, these already over-
whelming amounts could be substantially increased [as
they were] if, for instance OPEC were to force higher

prices [as it did] or if present oil company "participation agreements" with Middle Eastern governments were speeded up. Recent international monetary crises have shown vividly the dangers inherent in vast movements of currencies across national borders, so that the prospect of additional Middle Eastern billions being added to this movement is sobering indeed.

One must make a distinction, however, and a most important one, between the capital-poor oil producers who will invest the bulk of their oil revenues in imports and those that will accumulate a great surplus of funds. Countries such as Iraq, with a population of 10 million, Iran, with a population of 33 million, Nigeria, with a population of 55 million, and Indonesia, with a population of over 125 million will of necessity be exchanging their oil revenues for capital and consumer goods as well as technological services to be provided by the West, and they will thus create viable domestic economies for future generations.

On the other hand, countries such as Saudi Arabia, with a population of about 7 million, Kuwait with a population of 600,000, Libya, with a population of 2.5 million, and Abu Dhabi, with a population of 600,000, obviously will be receiving funds far in excess of what is needed to provide for the development of their people and their countries. They will be and now are investing abroad to establish other sources of income for the future to replace their declining oil revenues.

As we look ahead, then, it may well be surplus capital from these countries that will build oil refineries and subway systems in the United States, pipelines from the Arctic islands of Canada to the U.S. Midwest, tunnels under the English Channel, and new industries in Japan. The Saudi Arabian Minister of Petroleum, Sheik Yamani, has already proposed the building of oil refineries in the United States with Saudi Arabian funds. Certainly there are many appropriate channels for such investments—and a few inappropriate ones.

Efforts are also being made by OPEC members to pro-

94

cess their crude oil within their own borders and to rely on the consuming countries for markets only. Such a trend is sharply opposed in certain quarters for placing the consuming nations in altogether too vulnerable a position. If the refinery is located within the consuming area and difficulties develop in obtaining crude oil from a particular source, the consuming country can obtain it elsewhere. Should the refinery be located in a foreign area and if shipments are cut off, the consumer's ability to obtain the refined product elsewhere is critically limited. [Since 1974 the oil producers have increased their refinery capacity by about 250,000 barrels per day.]

In addition, it is hoped that the capital-rich members of OPEC will assist the developing Moslem countries with soft-money loans as well as their share of other world-wide foreign aid and disaster-relief programs.

Scylla and Charybdis

Thought has to be given to the potentially explosive political situation inherent in the Arab-Israel confrontation. Certainly, no easy solutions are in sight, but some elementary distinctions and recent oil-related developments are worth noting. Also, an examination of certain facts tends to alleviate to some extent one's natural uneasiness as to an ultimate conflict.

First, although the Middle East is overwhelmingly Moslem, it is not *all* Arab. The Arab oil world consists primarily of Iraq, Kuwait, Saudi Arabia, Qatar, Abu Dhabi, the small sheikdoms of the Trucial Coast, and the Arab oil-producing countries of North Africa, that is, Libya and Algeria.

Iran, with the world's second largest proven oil reserves (nearly 60 billion barrels) and a projected 1980 production of 8 to 10 million barrels per day, is not Arab and not a party to the Arab-Israel confrontation. It embraces the Moslem faith but has an entirely different ethnic origin than its Arab neighbors. It is not a part of

'Arab solidarity," and it is strongly pro-Western. In point of fact, more than one-third of the members of OPEC are non-Arab. Non-Arab lands, including Catholic Venezuela, Moslem Nigeria, and Indonesia, represent approximately 45 percent of OPEC's oil production and 25 percent of its reserves. This important distinction is frequently overlooked.

Furthermore, the parallel development of pipeline facilities and increasing oil production in Egypt and in Israel leads to a delicate "balance of vulnerability" and could provide a new mechanism for avoiding war.

Israel now has a major oil pipeline—the Trans-Israel Pipeline (TIPLINE)—running 160 miles from the gulf of Aqaba to the Mediterranean port of Ashkelon. Oilmen believe this pipeline is capable of handling at least 600,000 barrels of crude oil per day, with an ultimate capacity of 1.2 million. Egypt is constructing the Suez Mediterranean Pipeline (SUMED), running 207 miles from the Gulf of Suez to Alexandria, scheduled for completion by late 1974. Initial capacity is expected to be 800,000 barrels per day, with an ultimate capacity of between 1.6 and 2.5 million barrels per day. [The completed SUMED line has a capacity of 1.6 million barrels per day but only about one fourth of that capacity was being used in 1977.] Both TIPLINE and SUMED are highly vulnerable to destruction, yet neither has been disrupted so far. TIPLINE has been in operation since 1970, and SUMED under construction since 1971.

In addition to these vulnerable pipeline investments, Egypt's and Israel's oil production, while not at all comparable to the vast output of their neighbors, is still significant in terms of each country's domestic requirements. Several oil discoveries recently have been made in western Egypt which could prove to be significant, and production development in advancing there. Israel's oil comes from captured Sinai oil fields.

The vulnerability of these pipelines and oil production facilities actually serves to restrain both Egypt and

Israel from further conflict. Either side could destroy the other's facilities, but would inevitably suffer the loss of its own pipeline and production, hence, both are constrained from attack. It is, of course, a tenuous constraint. [Just how tenuous was demonstrated by the Yom Kippur War, which broke out several weeks after this paper was written and ended abruptly two weeks later. Neither pipeline was damaged in that crisis.] It is not, however, a negligible one, and perhaps provides only an economic incentive for peace. Also, it hardly need be pointed out that if any of the other Arab oil producing countries attacked Israel, their oil production facilities would invite an attack by the Israeli Air Force. It is hoped and expected that reason, negotiation, and mutual self-interest will resolve this difficult matter and that the existence of a balanced military deterrence will prevent an outbreak. This does not rule out, however the ever-present danger of pressure tactics in the form of imposing restrictions on oil production to influence the political balance. As a matter of fact, the existence of a balanced military deterrence tends to invite such pressures as the only power tool available to the parties concerned.

What We Can Do About It

Even assuming the uninterrupted flow of Middle East oil and a necessary and creative program of Middle Eastern investment in the consuming nations, the world must still learn to cope with the ultimate likelihood of declining oil reserves. This means simply that conservation policies must be adopted now, and that a full program of research and development of alternative energy resources must be implemented.

An initial first step would be the creation of a common oil policy on the part of the United States, Western Europe, and Japan to avoid the ill effects of individual consumer country bargaining. This would include (1) an oil consumers' union that would negotiate with OPEC for future supplies and would provide an effective basis for protecting the uninterrupted movement of oil; (2) the development of added supplies; (3) assurance of sufficient tanker and refining availability; (4) research into alternative sources of energy; and (5) provision for investment and tax incentives to stimulate these activities. Programs to reduce consumption must also be undertaken. The North Atlantic Assembly would do well to urge the adoption of such plans.

We must also note that coal is nature's most abundant energy resource and could be a far more important source of energy than it is. Coal is unfortunately a "dirty" fuel, and its mining is environmentally hazardous, but new methods exist for the conversion of coal into clean natural gas, and these should be perfected.

Every effort must be made toward the development of alternative energy resources such as controlled thermonuclear fusion, nuclear fission, solar energy, the harnessing of the tides, and geo-thermal power. Controlled thermonuclear fusion offers the best opportunity to obtain cheap and abundance energy consistent with high environmental standards. Collective international research and development could provide the world with ample alternative sources for heat and power, even if the automobile remains dependent on oil for its fuel. Collective efforts toward realization of these objectives could provide yet another area for mutual collaboration between all interested parties, including the Communist world.

Beyond all this, immediate action is required to restrict oil consumption. This calls for restrictions aimed at private automobile use and limitations on weight and engine size. Complementing this effort must be the expansion of fast urban mass-transit systems and intercity freight and passenger trains.

Taken together, these policy recommendations provide for both the short and long-term energy requirements of the world and will make full use of available resources. Moreover, these cooperative efforts should further reduce the likelihood of major conflicts. ◉

OBSERVATIONS ON U.S. AND INTERNATIONAL AFFAIRS INSPIRED BY WORLD CHANGES IN ENERGY COSTS

(1974)

In the aftermath of the Arab oil embargo, a long-range look at the problems of supply and cost.... Predicts that the oil shortages will prove temporary but that rising oil costs will have an abnormally strong impact on other costs and will restrict output and cause a recession.... Warns about fiscal policy and a future serious imbalance in our trade accounts.... Calls for smaller cars in the U.S..... Urges more aid from oil exporters to the less-developed countries, who face the greatest difficulties from the rising price of oil.... Asks again for governmental guidelines, because the profit motive alone will not solve the problem.

The recent oil consumers conference in Washington brings to mind the old description of how different nationalities face their problems: Given a serious problem, the French will add to it and the Germans will subtract from it; we Americans will multiply it—while the Scots take another drink and the English change the subject.

The energy crisis this winter gave us the opportunity to multiply our difficulties. Basically we face a temporary supply problem—which will be overcome soon— and a long-term price problem with rather overwhelming implications for inflation, the level of output and

Address to the University of Pennsylvania Executive Dinner, at the Wharton School. February 27, 1974.

100

employment, and finally, our international balance-of-payments problems. Our difficulties will be multiplied because of two Achilles heels inherent in our free-enterprise system. The balance-of-payments problem represents one of these vulnerable spots; the other is the fact that final-unit cost establishes the price for all production.

As a result of the latest increase, the price of imported oil is now nearly three times the average price of 1973. At these cost levels, the same volume that was imported last year would require an increase of about $60 billion in payments by the oil-importing countries in 1974. Although the price effects are being further aggravated by the Arab cutbacks and the embargo on shipments to the United States and the Netherlands, it seems evident that the embargo will be lifted shortly as a result of progress made on a Middle Eastern settlement. Supply, therefore, is not the real problem. The problem is exceptionally high cost.

In any event, there is good reason to believe that the new high prices and the pending Middle East settlement will soon induce a restoration of the pre-September production levels, and probably an even higher output.

Inflation

Increased energy costs will intensify world wide inflation, causing a decline of output and employment in the oil-importing countries. This decline may be so grat that measures taken to maintain economic activity may not entirely offset it, at least for the next several months.

The central point is that the inflationary impact cannot be limited to direct energy costs alone. These will naturally have to be passed on in higher prices for other consumer goods and services that require·inputs of energy. Thus, when the price of such an all-prevalent essential commodity as oil is sharply increased, an impetus is given to higher prices on literally everything, everywhere.

In the United States, we have had this experience superimposed on an already elevating price structure caused by the sale of one-fourth of our 1973 wheat crop to the Soviet Union. There also exists the danger that the sharp rise in the price of oil may encourage countries exporting other basic commodities to form their own cartels to fix higher prices. The extreme difficulties being encountered in the balance-of-payments area have compounded the problem by casting doubt over the long-term purchasing power of paper currency and have driven currency holders into commodities of all kinds as an inflation hedge, thus bringing about a skyrocketing rise in the world price level.

This brings us to one of the biggest weaknesses of the free-enterprise system, a weakness to which a democratic society is more vulnerable than a totalitarian one: the cost of bringing into production or acquiring the final unit of supply establishes the price for all production, regardless of cost.

Thus, the totalitarian countries purchases of the tail-end of their supply of wheat on the Western world's free markets establishes a price far above the average cost of wheat. Russia, China, and other such statist societies can mesh these prices with previous costs. In the United States, however, the entire crop is priced at the new levels. With our food production exposed to this threat on a scale far greater than heretofore, we can no longer afford to permit unlimited free access to our supply. If we do, we put the U.S. consumer, typically the housewife, in direct and disadvantageous competition with foreign governments.

Similarly, in a period of oil shortage, the selling price of our entire output is raised to a level to justify the search for new oil. Under normal circumstances these changes occur over a long enough period of time to permit a phasing in of the new price, but in periods of emergency, as now, controls are necessary.

In 1973, average hourly earnings in the United States rose by 6.7 percent in all private nonfarm employment, but *real* weekly wages fell by nearly 3 percent during this same period because consumer prices rose by 8.8 percent. The stabilization program prevented a larger rise in wages, but can labor be expected to absorb this year's greater and more dramatic rise in the cost of living without a corresponding increase in wages? Obviously not. [The consumer price index, based on 1967, rose from 133.1 in 1973 to 181.5 in 1977.]

From a social point of view no single force has a more corruptive and corrosive effect on a society than inflation, with its all-pervasive erosion of purchasing power and savings. As a matter of fact, history teaches us that when a country's inflation reaches a 15 percent level for three successive years, the result is a change in its form of government.

Output

We are finding out that the oil shortgage itself could be offset to a large extent by restricting consumption for driving and for heating, and by other conservation measures. This leaves an adequate supply for the production and transport of goods. The Council of Economic Advisors estimates that the higher price of oil may reduce consumer spending by about $12 billion in 1974 but will have a negligible effect on private investment and on net exports of goods and services. [In "constant dollar" terms, consumer spending declined by only 7 billion dollars in 1974 and has risen every year since then.]

In countries where imported oil is a larger part of total energy supply it is not possible to maintain supplies for transport and production, with the result that output will be much more severely affected. Thus, the Japanese government in its forecast for fiscal 1974 estimated that the growth of real GNP would be only 2.4

percent—the lowest in twenty years. Of greater concern to Japan, is a projected 17 percent increase in the price level.

Higher oil prices will bring about changes in the patterns of consumer spending and savings, and hence, investments. The reduction in aggregate demand probably will be considerably greater than the increase in the current payment to the oil-exporting countries. But it would only intensify inflation if, by means of easy fiscal and monetary policies, we attempted to expand aggregate demand by the *full* amount of the reduction induced by the higher cost of imported oil. The best that can be done through fiscal and monetary policies is to minimize the effects on output and employment so that recession will be mild.

Given time, the economy is expected to adjust to the change in the patterns of output and expenditure, and economic growth should be restored. There are 100 million automobiles and 20 million trucks in the United States. That is a vast captive market to be replaced as soon as possible with smaller cars and low-fuel-consumption engines.

Balance-of-Payments

As mentioned, the new prices will require an additional increase in payments to the oil-exporting countries of about $60 billion in 1974. Long-term methods of meeting such payments are yet to be devised. This is the other weakness of our society—the problem of transferring funds from one country to another. This problem is far greater than the difficulty of meeting the internal rise in the price of oil. The price rise might amount to between 1 percent and 5 percent but it might require up to 40 percent of the proceeds from exports to pay for it.

At the moment, the oil-producing countries are importing only what can be put in place in their own countries and investing the balance of their profits in short-term credit obligations. We can see the effect of that in the current decline in U.S. Treasury bill rates.

The payments "answer" cannot be found in fluctuating exchange rates, as some have contended. It would take an enormous depreciation of currency in some countries to increase exports and decrease imports sufficiently to offset their increased oil costs—and in a free market the depreciation of some currencies would soon be followed by competitive depreciations elsewhere.

One change on the horizon is a massive revaluation of gold by the central banks of the West. This would automatically increase the ability of the oil-importing countries to settle their accounts. Such dramatic changes in pricing are providing awkward, cumbersome, and sometimes bizarre solutions to the balance-of-payments problem. For example, we recently sold only thirty airplanes to Iran and priced them at $900 million.

The Developing Countries

If all these problems are difficult for the industrial countries, they are near-impossibilities for the developing ones. It is estimated that the cost of the less-developed countries' oil imports will rise from $5.2 billion in 1973 to $13—15 billion in 1974, and that their current account deficit for 1974 will be $24 billion, up from $10.6 billion in 1973. Such an increase in oil costs would be equivalent to 28 to 35 percent of LDC official reserve holdings, an amount equal to the total official bilateral flows of assistance financing to the developing world in 1972 of $8.6 billion. [In 1976, oil costs of non-producing LDCs reached $16 billion, which was 62 percent of their current account deficit of $25.8 billion.] LDCs are highly dependent on oil for growth.

In the Western Hemisphere, the LDCs get 74 percent of their energy from oil, and in the Eastern hemisphere,

58 percent. Unlike the developed world, these countries have very little nonessential consumption that can be curtailed without appreciably reducing output. The only solution is to increase aid. Without minimizing the moral obligation of the industrial countries to help, the *bulk* of this aid *must* come from the oil-exporting group, the only countries with any surplus funds for such purposes. In this connection, the Shah of Iran has offered to make 1 billion dollars available for loans to the developing countries at 7 to 8 percent interest—interest to be paid by the West. I cannot cheer over that, although Iran may be less able to help than, for example, Saudi Arabia.

Conclusion

The next few years will present a tremendous challenge to cope with these staggering difficulties. To a certain extent pure market forces will aid in solutions by spurring exploration and development of alternative energy resources and, one hopes, by shifting consumption and savings to more productive uses. But we must recognize in the West that the private sector alone cannot adapt our society to its new needs. While we must preserve the efficient competitive climate, we must inevitably expect a larger role for government in establishing enforceable guidelines for private enterprise.

But the greatest challenges lie in the area of organizing a more stable interdependence among the world's societies, in the creation of international institutions and arrangements to handle massive transfers of financial resources, and in the channeling of these resources into mutually beneficial investments. ◉

Postscript

Unfortunately, the predicted crisis in our balance-of-payments has engulfed us. The imbalance has occurred because we have not put a proper value on our role in the oil production-refining-

*distribution-consumption process. We have failed to bargain ade-
quately for our technology, our markets, and our enormously complex and capital-intensive facilities, all of which are necessary to
change the crude oil into a marketable product and move it to its
consumption points on a planetary-wide basis. We have pusillani-
mously engaged in the greatest peaceful transfer of wealth in
recorded history, and we now find ourselves unable to continue the
process without undermining the entire monetary system of the
west. Oil producers and oil consumers both stand to lose unless the
distortions are corrected.*

*Meanwhile, it would be better for us to pay more for oil domesti-
cally (by developing shale oil, for example) and keep the dollars at
home than to buy oil abroad at a lower price but suffer the consequent impact on our balance-of-payments.*

4
THE
NEED FOR
CAPITAL

The United States is usually thought of as a nation with an inexhaustible source of capital. Even before the 1973 oil crisis exacerbated the U.S. balance-of-payments problem, however, a long-term capital shortage was beginning to make itself felt. This shortage, with its concomitant evil of inflation, had its roots in the Vietnam War and added to the human, moral, and social distortions of that period.

In purely economic terms, not only did the war waste capital by expending vast sums for nonproductive purposes, but at the same time little effort was made to compensate for this outflow by reducing domestic spending.

The first of the two papers in this section, written in 1973, was one of the earliest public statements to point out that U.S. domestic needs—for energy, housing, and environmental protection, apart from other demands such as governmental deficits—would in the future transform the United States into a capital-short nation.

These two papers, spanning that great watershed of international economics, the 1973 oil crisis, were addressed to the growing capital shortage and to the remedies that might alleviate it. The first, "International Investment: A Two-Way Street," pointed out that American investment abroad was one cause of the capital shortage and proposed a greater investment in the United States by other countries. The article was written at a time when Canadians, in particular, and the French to a lesser degree, were complaining vigorously about the extent of U.S. control of their productive facilities.

The Canadian complaint was particularly pointless and unfair, given the fact that U.S. capital and accompanying technology had financed so many Canadian mines and industries and made an enormous contribution to the development of that nation, which otherwise might have remained longer in its frontier condition. Had the Canadians and others, instead of complaining, invested in turn in the United States, the world would be better off today, for interdependence is the key to economic progress and international political stability.

The second piece, testimony before the Congressional Sub-Committee on Economic Growth in May 1974, suggests domestic policies to alleviate the capital shortage. At the time that testimony was given the oil crisis was upon us and inflation was rampant. The foreign surpluses of dollars that had troubled the world economy the year before were in the process of shifting from the industrialized nations of the West to the oil-producing nations. For a time, that shift made more capital available to the United States as the oil producers deposited much of their accumulations in American banks. But that provided only temporary relief as new problems arose.

INTERNATIONAL INVESTMENT: A TWO-WAY STREET

(1973)

A plea for more direct European investment in U.S. production facilities....Differences of attitude between U.S. and European investors...

A greater degree of direct foreign investment in the U.S. would help solve the balance-of-payments problem, provide a healthy stimulus to U.S. industry, and create, through interdependence, more international understanding.

In the last few years domestic spokesmen in labor and other fields have joined foreigners in criticizing overseas investment by corporations. The criticism concentrates on the negative aspects of multinational business: the possibilities for economic imperialism, added difficulties for the international monetary system, and unilateral allocations of employment opportunities.

The criticism appears to overlook the solid productive performance of international investment which has meant, in simple terms, a more abundant life for more people around the globe. Many of the problems critics wish to see resolved by controls or protectionism might find solutions if positive aspects of international investment were better appreciated and if the United States itself were to become, to a greater extent, the host country for foreign investment in productive facilities.

One of the most often cited indicators of imbalance in the world economy is the U.S. balance-of-payments position. In the last decade, when the U.S. payments deficit has averaged something under $3 billion a year, the United States has been investing abroad at the rate

This article, in slightly different form, appeared in the *Columbia Journal of World Business*, Spring 1973.

of about $10 billion a year. If foreign investment in the United States had even approached the level of U.S. investment abroad, the balance-of-payments deficit would have been countered. [Since 1972, U.S. investment abroad has continued to grow at a faster rate than foreign investment in the U.S.]

More important than increasing the absolute level of foreign investment in the United States is the composition of that investment. At present this reflects an intense preference for liquidity. Foreign investment in the United States totaled some $123 billion in 1971 [$265 billion in 1976], and over half of this, $73 billion [$180 billion in 1976], was short-term investment and a further $36 billion [$55 billion] was invested in portfolio securities. Looked at the other way, "direct" investment accounts for 50 percent of the U.S. investment abroad and only 11 percent of foreign investment in the U.S. [This relationship has changed for the better since then.]

The marked European liquidity preference undoubtedly stems from a combination of factors. For a long time economic and political uncertainty and a somewhat lesser state of economic development made European investors liquidity conscious, and certainly the loss of private fixed investments in two world wars made liquid assets attractive. These experiences were heightened by a long history of gaps in governmental financial credibility in Europe, with numerous examples of complete failures in currency systems which made Europeans distrustful of holding their own currency. Moreover, under widely prevailing exchange-control systems, nonresident accounts—including the foreign-currency deposits of European nationals—are accorded much greater freedom than is given to resident accounts.

The essential difference, however, between European and U.S. investors appears to be that Europeans think of direct investment in terms of being "high risk" whereas Americans think of it in terms of "high productivity" and, therefore, "high profits." This is an important attitudinal difference: cash balances are themselves more risky than solid balance-sheet assets.

If this liquidity preference could be overcome, the volume of volatile short-term funds that now generate crises would be sharply reduced and the volume of funds committed to more stable production uses would be increased.

In fact, present imbalancing movements of funds appear large only in the context of individual country reserves. Applying almost any velocity multiplier to the Eurocurrency market, for instance, would suggest that normal international business activities require a level of transactions much higher than the recent "hot money" flows of about $25 billion. Monetary reform directed towards eliminating rather than accommodating such flows is likely to be ineffectual. Meanwhile, a healthier pattern in the employment of funds in the United States would help offset imbalancing movements of funds.

Apart from such balance-of-payments and monetary stability considerations, there are other reasons for the United States to welcome increased foreign investment.

At a time when Americans are concerned about corporate economic hardening-of-the-arteries and concentration of decision-making power, constructive competititon in the domestic economy would be increased by foreign investment in direct productive facilities.

With increased investment would come a welcome stimulation of the flow of other technologies. One feels constrained to remind both the United States and other nations of the impressive technological contributions made to the body of Western technology by many diverse countries. The range is wide: everything from electrodialysis (Germany) to the contact lens (Japan), from radial tires (France) to radar (Great Britain), from holography (Hungary) to DDT (Switzerland). International investment encourages the synchronization of technology and promotes, through competititon, a

113

constantly improving technological base, worldwide in scope and benefit.

The United States, highly developed though it is, will in all probability be a capital-absorbing economy in the period of immense and urgent capital requirements, and U.S. capital outflow is likely to slow down because of domestic needs. The requirements for energy, housing, urban renovation and environmental protection and reconstruction will place tremendous calls on capital. In fact, certain economic evaluations indicate that the general amount needed for environmental purposes alone may soon reach a substantial portion—perhaps a third—of the country's gross national product within the next decade. These requirements are the forerunners of greatly heightened business activity in the years ahead and make this a particularly appropriate time for further foreign investment in the United States.

Finally, increased foreign experience with direct investment in the United States would create among critics of U.S. corporations abroad a greater understanding of the mutual advantages of overseas investment. In his *Le Défi Americain*, Jean-Jacques Servan-Schreiber eloquently expressed his concern over the degree of U.S. management of European industry. In contrast, it is clear that the United States would welcome additional foreign direct investment and greater participation in the U.S. economy. International investment gives both parties a better understanding of each other's economic needs and, in so doing, helps harmonize world society.

The advantages of increased foreign investment in the United States would not all accrue to the United States. Such an increase would provide a constructive use for accumulated dollar reserves and, in so doing, would in effect remove the so-called "overhang" of "surplus" dollars held in European and Japanese central banks. Furthermore, earnings derived from productive facilities build added and continuing exchange strength on capital accounts comparable to that enjoyed by the

United States.

An increase in the flow of foreign investment into the United States and, more important, a revision of the pattern of that investment would be welcome, beneficial, and productive for all concerned. Once the flows of U.S. investment abroad and foreign investment into the United States become more nearly balanced, an important crisis-producing circumstance which has wracked the international monetary system in recent years would be eased considerably. Essentially, this is because the U.S. balance-of-payments deficit and other countries' corresponding surpluses could be readily countered by increased foreign investment in the United States.

Overseas investment should be encouraged by all governments by all available means. The rapid increase in European monetary and currency controls is deeply disturbing as a major menace to the free and integrated West that we have all come so far in building. Japan also remains remarkably closed off by controls, despite gargantuan surpluses.

Ours is an intensely interdependent world, and international investment and production are crucial to the genuine unification of world society. When the objectives are socially oriented as well, they provide efficient solutions for the world's ever-growing consumption needs and bring together creative world forces in undertakings for mutual benefit. ◉

Postscript

Since this paper was written the strength of European currencies relative to the dollar has encouraged a sharp increase in direct foreign investment in the United States and thus heightened the international community's concern for our stability.

European-based corporations have taken over, or bought substantial ownership in, a number of American firms: Unilever, N.V., bought Lipton Tea and National Starch and Chemical; Cavenham of the U.K. purchased Grand Union; Bauer took over Miles Laboratories; British-American Tobacco bought Gimbels; and British Oxygen increased its share of Airco. As the result of these and a number of other major investments, direct foreign investment in the United States has increased 19 percent a year between 1972 and 1976, compared to an increase of only 13 percent a year for all categories of foreign investment. During the same period U.S. direct investment abroad increased by only 11 percent a year.

THE
CAPITAL CRISIS
AND HOW TO MEET IT
(1974)

*An outline of the capital shortage in the U.S.
and its causes....A defense of corporate profits as
essential for the provision of new and needed
capital....Specific recommendations, including
increased capital recovery tax allowances,
inflation credits for savers and investors, new
supportive policies on the part of regulatory agencies, and the suggestion that corporations be permitted to deduct from taxes what they pay out in
dividends.*

The capital shortage, like the oil shortage, has been
building up for some time. The present crunch has its
roots in the vast capital investment in the Vietnam War
and the failure to reduce domestic spending during that
period. The erosion of our capital base started there,
and during this period were sown the seeds of inflation.

The float of the dollar on August 15, 1971, with its
inflationary impact, the 1972 failure of the Russian and
Chinese wheat crops and the Soviet purchases of grains
in our markets, the bizarre but tragic disappearance of
anchovies—an important protein source in cattle
feed—off the Peruvian Coast, the further devaluation of
the dollar in February 1973, and finally the Mideast War
and the leap forward in energy costs, resulted in a star-
tling rise in 1973 of 13.1 percent in the Wholesale Price
Index compared to only 4½ percent in 1972. It is now
expected that the increase for 1974 will exceed that of
last year. [It did: 18.9 percent.] I expect a significant sub-
siding in the inflationary rate next year [9.2 percent in
1975], but it will rest at a level substantially higher than
heretofore. The battle to hold inflation to the 2 to 3 per-

Statement before the Sub-Committee on Economic Growth, Joint Economic Committee, U.S. Congress, May 8, 1974.

cent level of the decades of the 1950s and 1960s has no doubt been lost.

It is now urgently necessary for our capital base to be increased to make possible the replacement of existing facilities and the financing of new plant additions whose production will in time quench the fires of inflationary demand. The challenge is to repair and improve our capital markets so that once again they can carry out their proper functions.

The Role of the Corporation

The corporation—that ingenious instrument of English jurisprudence—with its immortality, creativity, and efficiency, has provided us with the means to satisfy consumer needs on a scale unequalled by those societies that have adopted a different economic system.

In order to survive—let alone progress—corporations are driven by powerful forces outside their own control to spend vast sums in order to maintain their property accounts, to remain competitive, to meet ever-rising labor rates, and finally to finance inventories which sponge up inflated dollars. This intense struggle to keep up is too often unseen and unknown to the general public and even the opinion makers.

It is obvious that a few companies, in their overzealous pursuit of profit, have been callously indifferent to social objectives, and others have violated proper business and legal codes. But we shall not condemn the innocent with the guilty; this is not the time for panic about the failure of our free enterprise system.

The capstone of our system is the nation's process of capital formation—via savings institutions, life insurance companies, private pension plans, and retained earnings on the part of corporate society. This process commands worldwide respect—particularly from those that live under other economic systems that do

118

not create such capital pools and who therefore are most anxious to tap ours.

Corporate profit has become a bad word, despite the fact that it is through retained profits, thriftily reinvested in the business by stockholders rather than taken out in dividends, that corporations largely finance their needs. For every dollar retained, our companies may borrow as much again for plant, equipment, and working capital.

There is a strong tendency to think that profits are something a business does not really need, or at least something that can be reduced without serious consequences. This is irresponsible, because these earnings are the essential elements in capital formation.

What Can Be Done?

Corporate capital recovery allowances should be increased.

At the present time, U.S. investment in productive facilities, as a percentage of GNP, is the lowest of the major industrialized countries: our ratio is 10 percent, while Japan's, for example, is 20 percent. No wonder capital investments have been declining during the last ten years from $52,000 to $42,000 per worker.

The United States also has the highest percentage of obsolete production facilities of any of the leading industrial nations, and a relatively low capital recovery tax allowance. Under U.S. tax laws it generally takes ten and half years to write off capital costs; enterprises in the United Kingdom can recover their costs in one year, in Canada two years, Italy six, Sweden five, and West Germany nine. Sweden, which is supposed to be socialist and therefore less supportive of business, enjoys one of the highest cost recovery allowances, permitting a writeoff of 130 percent in seven years, thus providing an added incentive to corporate investment.

After seven years U.S. business can write off only 88.5 percent of capital costs [since increased to 94.5 percent].

Inflation protection for savers, investors, and corporations.

We have come to accept cost-of-living pay increases as an integral part of American labor contracts and we are moving in that direction for all fixed-income benefits. In other words, we are beginning to accept inflation as a reality. But surely this concept and these kinds of benefits ought to be extended to some degree to savers and investors, and to industries as well. I do not recommend that we follow Brazil's extensive and exhaustive pattern of price-level indexing (which allows fixed assets to be revalued according to an inflation index, thus accelerating depreciation write-offs). We would no doubt have to give up many of our democratic concepts and freedoms to make the Brazilian program work in the United States. Besides, Brazil does not play a major role in the world's economy, as we do; any steps we take in the direction of price-level indexing would have to be studied carefully for the impact they would have on our trading partners and the world at large.

Some protection against inflation, however, must be provided for those who still hold to the virtues of thrift. Paul McCracken has suggested that the personal exemptions and bracket limits of the personal income tax could be adjusted automatically for changes in the consumer price index and that the government could obligate itself to pay holders of savings bonds a contractual "real" rate.

Regulatory agencies should be supportive.

In full view of Congress, our federal regulatory agencies have undermined, and in some cases destroyed, vast segments of our corporate society. This is because of the agencies' inability to understand the role of profits in the maintenance and development of the economic areas under their control.

In particular, the Interstate Commerce Commission, with its unbelievably protracted hearings, has helped force much of our railroad industry into receivership: contemplate, if you will, the absurdity of twelve years of hearings on the Rock Island merger. The railroad industry presently earns 3 percent on its capital and so, of course, is cut off from any new equity money.

The Civil Aeronautics Board, in its obsession with enforced duplication of facilities and low fares, has brought the airlines to the verge of bankruptcy. The debt of the five largest U.S. airlines is now $4 billion, almost three times what it was ten years ago. Five of our eight major trunkline carriers are unable to pay dividends, and the market value of seven of these eight carriers is only 79 percent of their original book values.

Modify the tax structure.

It is unfair to subject corporate earnings to taxes at three different levels—the 48 percent corporate earnings tax, the tax on dividends to recipients and, finally, the capital gains tax. Britain permits companies to deduct from taxes what they pay out in dividends. This allows companies to distribute larger dividends, which makes stock investment more attractive, while still retaining earnings for capital expansion. Why should not the United States adopt similar policies?

The [present] proposals to reduce capital gains taxes and holding periods deserve careful Congressional attention. I do believe, though, that these proposals are inadequate, and that the schedule of reductions is too protracted. The patient must not die on the operating table. As we agree that ultimate redress in these taxes is the goal, I strongly urge that the problem be fully rectified at the outset. Saving must be made more attractive than spending.

Structural changes needed in our securities markets

Congress has before it important legislation dealing with structural changes in the securities markets.

I find the proposals to prohibit pension funds from

owning more than 5 percent of any one company most attractive. I think they are essential to breaking up the excessive concentration of institutional stock ownership in a relatively few giant corporations.

I would strongly oppose attempts to do away with over-the-counter and third-market transactions; these efficient dealings are necessary for competition.

I believe the commission price structure needs drastic overhauling. Institutions pay about 0.4 percent commission for the purchase and sale of shares; similar transactions by individuals are burdened with a charge of approximately four percent. No wonder the number of stockholders in our American enterprises declined by 800,000 in 1972 and by the same number again in 1973. [It is still declining, down 18 percent between 1970 and 1975, and there is evidence of another 10 percent decline since then.]

Congress should compensate for present monetary policy.

The Federal Reserve Board's monetary policy might well extend the period of inflation and have a disastrous effect on our capital markets, unless offsetting steps are taken by Congress. The Board's present policy of limiting money growth to 6.6 percent, in an attempt to lean heavily against this year's expected inflationary price rise of over 15 percent, might be appropriate if that were our only problem.

We are, however, faced with the additional formidable difficulties of raising this year $30 billion for private account in the bond and stock markets and of raising upwards of $200 billion in equity money alone in the next ten years. With soaring interest rates that will be impossible, and without a strong and buoyant capital market, the country will be unable to build the facilities necessary to halt the rising prices of raw materials and manufactured goods.

In planning for the future, the government must establish the social objectives and goals of our nation and the sound economic framework within which they are to be achieved. Priorities cannot be determined by the profit motive alone, but our corporations, rightly spurred on by economic incentives, can help us realize our vision of a better society. ◉

Postscript

Little has been done toward tax reform as suggested in this paper. In fact, further retrogressive measures have been enacted, such as lengthening the holding period for capital gains from six months to one year. Other tax reform proposals would alter our tax structure adversely, putting a greater burden on corporations, and thus damaging the long-term interests of the country.

Risk-bearing is an essential element of the developmental process and the accumulation of capital for this purpose should be encouraged.

5

EAST-WEST TRADE: THE PATH TO PEACE

The three papers in this section span a decade of profound changes in the relationship between the industrialized West and the Communist bloc. Underlying all three articles, however, is a common theme: International trade and the interdependence that grows out of it represent the best guarantees of peace.

"What Next for NATO?" dates from 1966, a time when the world was still chilled by the distrust and suspicion of the Cold War. It was written with the hope that NATO could do more than provide a military shield for the West; it urged NATO to take positive political and economic steps to increase East-West understanding and cooperation, and thus lessen the chances of war.

Significantly, the paper also called attention to a fact that few people were then considering but that has now become common wisdom: namely, that the economic problems of the less-developed countries present as great a threat to peace as does the political division of Europe.

By 1970, when "The Ties that Bind" was written, trade between the Communist bloc and the NATO nations had made a modest beginning, and tensions in Europe were easing slightly. Analyzing the structural differences that limited economic relations between

East and West, the paper pointed out that East-West trade could attain the level of its natural economic potential only if Western lending institutions—and Western governments—made large amounts of credit available.

Indeed, events since then have borne out this view. Credits *were* offered and trade levels have more than tripled as a result, with beneficial results for both sides.

As is often the case, however, that success has engendered new problems, which are the subject of the last paper in this section. Although the peace seems firmer today, the possibility of nuclear war is still with us. "Dueling and Dealing with the Russians" was written in 1977; it suggests a policy by which credits and trade can be utilized to bring about disarmament and thus eliminate the final awesome threat.

WHAT NEXT FOR NATO?

(1966)

An early suggestion that NATO supplement its military role with more constructive political and economic tasks in the interest of East-West integration....NATO is more militant than its individual members.

NATO has been an extremely successful undertaking. No alliance of its size and scope has ever before existed in history. But it is clearly time to question some of its fundamentals; the more closely we scrutinize NATO the more it seems that basic changes must take place if the organization is to survive and maintain its vitality.

These changes should reflect present day realities. I propose that NATO begin to deemphasize its primary military and defensive aspects, assume a more active and purposeful role in the political arena—a task for which it is ideally suited—and reduce somewhat its military expenditures to allow member countries to make significantly larger contributions toward their own well being and towards the economic and social welfare of the underdeveloped world.

NATO, broadly speaking, has been the victim of its own success. It was so well conceived that it has tended naturally to keep traveling on its original course, thus projecting, year after year, the same aggressive military posture that it adopted out of necessity at its birth. NATO was founded sixteen years ago as an appropriate response to the Soviet Union's militant and expansionist ambitions in Europe. NATO preserved the balance of power in Europe and permitted its members to recover from the devastation of World War II and to develop strong economies and internal political stabil-

Presented to the Committee on the Reform of NATO, NATO Parliamentarians' Conference. Paris, November 15, 1966.

ity. It was a military alliance fitted to a particular time and set of conditions—most of which no longer exist. Thus, NATO today represents a somewhat wasteful and potentially dangerous over-reaction to the present international situation.

The concept of mutual cooperation in defense, as embodied in Article V of the North Atlantic Treaty, is still valid: "An attack on one country will be considered an attack on all." We must remain committed to this vital principle. But while some defensive posture will have to be maintained for the foreseable future, it can be reduced to levels more consistent with the current situation. The massive size and sophistication of the NATO military arsenal could be reduced unilaterally without subjecting member countries to risk. The Cold War began in Europe, it first thawed in Europe, and perhaps it can be soonest ended there.

But if NATO is to reduce its military commitments to levels more consistent with the current state of affairs, will it not then be foretelling its own dissolution? Not at all. Purely military objectives will give way to wider horizons. The reasonable and legitimate military considerations that continue to exist will be properly satisfied only if NATO is reunified through the pursuit of broader political objectives.

It is no longer in our interest to isolate Eastern Europe. Instead, what is needed is an integrated relationship, with the United States and the Soviet Union cooperating to guarantee Europe's future. We must have an organization that will bind together Western and Eastern Europe. So far, NATO has done nothing towards this end—not for want of opportunity, but because of the limitations and inhibitions imposed at the outset. Such limitations currently make NATO a divisive rather than a constructive force.

NATO itself is far more militant than its individual members, who, independently and despite the existence of NATO, practice coexistence with Russia and the Eastern European nations. Yet, there is a limit to the rapprochement that we can achieve while NATO's weapons are pointed at those with whom we attempt to have closer ties.

NATO is making no significant contribution towards resolving one of the basic issues left over from World War II: the problem of German unification. It might be argued that these criticisms are misdirected, for NATO was never constituted to assume such a task. They are raised here because it is essential that some multinational organization take on these important responsibilities.

Although a case can be made for setting up an entirely new structure to meet these objectives, there are good reasons for giving the job to NATO. Over the years, strong lines of communication between member countries have been established and tested, under sometimes difficult circumstances, and they have endured. For example, the tremendously complex business of sharing costs has been worked out by continuous negotiation. The United States, for instance, contributed approximately 44 percent of the cost of the infrastructure projects in the early 1950s, in contrast to the 1966 contribution of 24.8 percent. The United Kingdom reduced its contribution from 27 percent initially to 13 percent currently. In the meantime, the Continental nations increased their payments: Italy raised her share from 5.7 percent in 1951 to 6.6 percent. West Germany, which was allocated a 13.7 percent share of costs when it first joined NATO, now contributes 21.9 percent. [These shares have not changed significantly since 1966.] NATO members have also shared technical, scientific, and economic information in significant areas.

We should take this collective experience and expand it to create a regional entity that would be effective in all phases of political, economic, and cultural life. Such an undertaking would not be financially onerous. NATO's organizational costs, as distinct from military support and equipment furnished by member nations, were $213 million in 1965. In comparison, the organizational costs of the United Nations were only $108.5 million last year. [Consider what NATO could do organizationally with its economic resources if its military goals were broadened to include social objectives.]

In short, I am proposing that NATO be continued as a regional military alliance for mutual cooperation — with broader objectives. These new objectives would not place the organization in conflict with any existing international organization; they would merely allow NATO to give valuable and necessary help.

Let us examine some of the important economic consequences of a cut in NATO's military expenditures. The defense budgets of the NATO members totaled $74.2 billion in 1965. The Warsaw Pact countries had a combined defense budget of $43 billion, of which $40 billion was contributed by the Soviet Union. [NATO and Warsaw Pact defense expenditures are now roughly equal.] Of last year's total defense budget of $74 billion for NATO members, it is reliably estimated that about $30 billion was the cost of keeping up the military readiness of NATO itself. This is a staggering sum to pay to maintain a strong military stance that, though once necessary, has been made obsolete by history.

Needless to say, any reduction in NATO's military spending would allow for immense social and economic gains within NATO countries. Member countries also would have funds freed for larger contributions to existing international organizations. In 1965, the budget of the World Health Organization was only $39 million, that of UNESCO, $24 million, and for the Food and Agriculture Organization, merely $19.3 million. [These budgets have increased up to ten-fold but still fall within the same order of magnitude as NATO military costs.] The World Food Program of FAO, begun in 1966, raised pledges of only $208 million worth of food for the period 1966 through 1968. Contrast these figures with the $30 billion for NATO's annual military expenditures.

In today's world, the major political tensions are no

longer primarily those between Western and Eastern Europe. In fact, there is visible and substantial evidence that the future challenge lies in the backward areas of the world—Latin America, Africa, Southeast Asia, and, overshadowing all else, Communist China. The abysmal poverty and consequent political instability of many underdeveloped countries constitute a much greater threat to world peace than we encounter in Europe.

A redirected NATO would produce three principal benefits. First, the North Atlantic Treaty Organization itself, with its established areas of cooperation and a well-trained and experienced secretariat, could play a leading role in solving some of the outstanding problems of Europe. Second, if NATO reduced its military spending, member countries could consequently invest more heavily in their domestic welfare programs. Third, funds released from NATO military commitments would allow for increased contributions to international organizations and aid to underdeveloped nations. NATO therefore has in its grasp the power to promote and encourage a three-pronged attack on some of the most pressing problems of our time. If we seize these opportunities, NATO's role in the future will be as valuable as the role it has played in the past. ◉

THE
TIES THAT BIND
(1970)

A call for an increase in East-West trade to ease the tensions of the Cold War....Describes the obstacles to this trade and suggests that governmental credits and tax incentives could help overcome them....Discusses various forms of trade agreements with the Soviet bloc and welcomes the beginnings of trade with China.

The most promising opportunity for easing the strains between the NATO countries and their Eastern European counterparts lies in accelerating the growth of trade between these two great areas. Trade intertwines the self-interests of both sides and promotes interdependence, an important bulwark of stability.

Russia, with its population of 239 million, and the other Eastern European countries, with a combined population of 120 million, provide a well-organized market of 360 million educated people, many of whom come from backgrounds similar to those of their counterparts in Western Europe. East bloc countries have a good record of fulfilling their contracts with Western corporations. Business law and business ethics in the Communist world are surprisingly similar to those in the West, despite the fundamental structural differences in business organizations and the differing theoretical assumptions regarding the social functions of business activity and commerce. These countries exceed the Common Market's population of 200 million and are not far behind it in productivity and consumption. Nevertheless, only 4 percent of all the foreign trade of the members of NATO is with this great trading area.

Trade among the nations of the Free World is expected to continue to grow at close to the 10–15 percent rate that it has averaged over the last fifteen years; such

Paper presented to the Political and Economic Committees, North Atlantic Assembly. The Hague, October 1970.

trade is well-established and relatively mature. In contrast, trade with the Eastern bloc is only marginally familiar to most business and government exporting organizations in the West. An increase in this trade should be an important NATO goal.

Some Obstacles

There are three major differences between NATO's trade with Communist bloc countries and its trade with other countries.

● Eastern bloc business transactions are consummated by government organizations whose decisions are often affected as much by political as by economic considerations.

● Many Communist nations are not members of the General Agreement of Tariffs and Trade (GATT). A Western country may have a bilateral trade agreement with a Communist country and need not grant Communist countries most-favored-nation tariff status.

● For most members of NATO, trade with the Eastern bloc is governed by the Coordinating Committee (COCOM) list of some 160 strategic commodities— (for example, computers)—that may not be exported to Communist countries. Items embargoed from export to Communist China are on the so-called CHINCOM list.

Despite these obstacles, trade between NATO members and the East has grown at a rapid percentage rate from an extremely low base. NATO exports to eastern Europe, including the Soviet Union, rose from $1.1 billion in 1957 to $4.1 billion in 1968. During the same periods, imports from eastern Europe increased from $1.1 billion to $3.9 billion. [In 1976 NATO exported $23.3 billion worth of goods to the East bloc and imported $17.9 billion.]

NATO members are already taking some steps

to enlarge their trading with the East. These include credits, tax incentives, and bilateral trade agreements.

Credit

Practically all trade requires credit arrangements. Without them trade can advance little beyond the level of barter. International trade involves such difficulties and risks that credit to the buyer or seller or both, and some kind of insurance for the seller, become almost essential. An international transaction takes a long period of time to complete. During that time the buyer's or seller's circumstances or the political and economic conditions in either country may change. The risks are well known: insolvency of one party, devaluation, confiscation, war, revolution, changes in import regulations, and loss or damage to goods in transit. The longer the time required the greater the risk, so these factors bear most acutely on the export of specially manufactured capital goods. In addition, and again particularly with capital goods, the buyer by necessity wishes to defer payment.

To meet these needs, all governments have set up agencies that either grant credit directly to exporters or rediscount a major part of the credit granted to exporters by banks or other private financial institutions. They have also established official or quasi-official agencies that insure export credits.

Financing is such an important competitive tool in promoting exports that the major industrial countries, through the Berne Union, have set up guidelines limiting the amount of government-supported financing. However, the line between commercial export financing, which is subject to the limitations set up by the Berne agreements, and the financing of development projects, which is not, is not clear. In France, Italy, the United Kingdom, and West Germany—but not in the

United States—medium-term commercial and government interest rates are significantly lower for exports than they are for domestic borrowers. There is little doubt that on major projects interest rates are modified and repayment schedules are extended well beyond the five-year limit set by the Berne Union.

The importance of credit as a competitive tool in promoting exports is hardly open to question, yet little statistical evidence has ever been put together to weigh its effect. The fact that the U.S. Export-Import Bank does not finance trade with Communist countries provides an opportunity of comparing trade levels where there is government-supported credit and where there is not. Such figures can at best provide only tentative evidence, but they indicate that government-supported financing can as much as double exports of major capital goods.

There are also indications that direct government grants of credit and government guarantees or rediscounting of credit generate additional, unsupported export business. This can be demonstrated by comparing the level of actual exports with the level of government-supported export credits over a period of years. One such comparison shows that over a four-year period thirteen Western industrialized countries consistently exported three dollars worth of heavy and electrical machinery to the Eastern bloc for every dollar of credits they granted for that category of exports. Clearly, continued improvement of credit, insurance, and guarantees of export financing can significantly promote trade with the Communist nations—as well as with the rest of the world.

Tax Incentives

One of the problems in promoting exports is that it is more attractive for a company to sell in its home market than to cope with all the problems of language, foreign regulations, currency, and credit checking that are involved in export operations.

Exporting can be made more profitable by exempting export profits from certain taxes. A great advantage of the value added tax is the nearly automatic refund of taxes on exported goods. All indirect taxes have similar advantages over income and other direct taxes. Among NATO countries, the United States, Canada, and the United Kingdom rely most heavily on direct taxes. The United Kingdom has made a series of complicated exceptions and adjustments to its tax schedules to promote exports; the United States and Canada have thus far done very little. In fact, the U.S. tax system in some ways discourages exports: by deferring income tax liability on certain foreign profits, it encourages U.S. corporations to set up manufacturing subsidiaries abroad rather than to export U.S.-made goods.

In 1970, however, the Treasury proposed to allow U.S. corporations to set up a new type of subsidiary to be called a Domestic International Sales Corporation (DISC). To qualify as a DISC company, the subsidiary would have to derive at least 95 percent of its income from export sales or activities ancillary to such sales, including interest received on any credit extended to finance its export sales. Ninety-five percent of the DISC company assets would also have to be related to export activities.

The profits of a DISC firm would not be subject to U.S. income tax until they were distributed to the parent company. In addition, where the U.S. parent company manufactures the products that the DISC company exports, the Internal Revenue Service would allow a greater allocation of profits to the DISC company than the present arms-length allocation rules allow. The Treasury estimates that under its proposal, DISC companies could defer all their income taxes for a minimum of ten years and that DISC companies whose profits were growing could defer all their income taxes for longer than that. [The DISC proposal became law but, unfortunately, its tax provisions were abused, and in 1977 consideration was being given to phasing it out.]

Other countries have authorized similar tax-favored entities to promote exports. Such tax-forgiving measures can encourage all overseas trade, with particular benefit to trade with the East, which has been so neglected.

Bilateral Trade Agreements

GATT, to which all NATO members belong, forbids any member to enter into a trade arrangement with any one member nation that it does not offer to every other member nation. There are a few exceptions, but that is the basic element in the system of multilateral trade that GATT is designed to encourage. However, the Communist countries are not GATT members, and a major part of the trade of NATO members with Eastern bloc countries is carried on under bilateral agreements. [Czechoslovakia, Hungary, Rumania, and Poland are now members of GATT.]

These bilateral agreements are not much better than extended barter arrangements. Some consist of precise contracts covering carefully described exchanges of specified amounts of goods. At the other extreme, some are merely statements of intent to exchange a certain value of goods over a period of time. Most lie somewhere in between, enumerating the goods each side intends to ship and setting forth pricing and arbitration rules. In general, these agreements are primitive, cumbersome, inflexible, and far less economic in their use of productive resources than a multilateral trading system. Nevertheless, since the Communist countries have so far not chosen to join the complex of treaties that make up the trading system of the West, such bilateral arrangements must provide the basic framework for trade with the East.

A recent trend in these agreements combines trade

with financing. Probably the best publicized is the agreement between West Germany and the Soviet Union under which West German manufacturers are supplying the Soviet Union with large-diameter steel pipe. A consortium of German banks is financing a major part of the purchase price, and the government is guaranteeing the loan. Payment will be made through the pipe itself, by delivery of natural gas to Germany between 1973 and 1993.

In a similar transaction, English contractors have undertaken to build a $3 million irrigation project in Rumania. It is being financed by British banks, with the financing guaranteed by the Export Credits Guarantee Department of the government. Payment is to be made in agricultural products grown at the irrigation site.

Clearly, there are opportunities for creative salesmanship and financing on a bilateral basis; perhaps the surface has just been scratched. But note again the awkwardness of working out a deal like this for each transaction, compared to the simplicity of the normal money contract that is basic to a multilateral trade system.

Imports, Tariffs, and Quotas

One factor inhibiting trade with the Eastern bloc nations has been their policy of keeping exports to and imports from each country in approximate balance. This, of course, limits Eastern bloc trade to the low level that can be accomplished in a series of bilateral agreements. The contrast with the more productive and efficient trade made possible under the free world's multilateral system is striking. It appears, however, that country-by-country balanced trade will remain one of the adverse conditions that traders with the East will have to accept. [This has changed.]

Since the Communist countries are not members of GATT, their exports to GATT members do not automatically receive most-favored-nation tariff treatment. This can be significant. In the United States, for instance, imports from countries not receiving most-favored-nation status are subject to the much higher rates of the Smoot-Hawley Act of 1930. The Communist nations also set differing tariffs for different countries. However, bilateral agreements can modify the tariff rates for individual commodities in particular instances. Furthermore, since Soviet purchasing policy is often governed by factors other than economic, prices can be adjusted to offset or increase the effect of any tariff.

Recent trading patterns suggest that Eastern bloc countries prefer to trade where the tariff barriers against their commodities are lower. Since any attempt to increase exports to Communist countries must allow for an increase in imports as well, this may require a planned reduction in tariffs and other barriers.

In practice, this planning has sometimes appeared to be negative. On several occasions NATO members negotiated bilateral agreements with Communist countries providing for the exchange of groups of named commodities—and then the Western country placed a quota on one of the commodities that it had agreed to import. These quotas were apparently designed to prevent the importing country from becoming too dependent on a single source of supply. Such actions may not violate the letter of the prior trade agreements, but they severely strain their spirit. Future trade would be better served by recognizing the limitations at the outset.

Some Hopeful Developments

The U.S. government seems to be moving toward a more positive policy on trade with Communist countries. The Export Administration Act of 1969 directs the Secretary of Commerce to review the list of prohibited commodities and to remove those items of which the export may no longer present a threat to the national security. In making such determination, the Secretary is to consider whether such commodities are available to Communist countries from other non-Communist sources, a consideration that was explicitly excluded from the previous law. Less tangible, but possibly more significant, the promotion of foreign trade is declared to be the goal of the legislation; limiting that trade to protect the national security is stated second, as an exception. Furthermore, in September 1970, the United States Treasury ceased requiring foreign subsidiaries of U.S. corporations to obtain a Treasury permit in addition to the basic Export Control permit when exporting to a Communist country.

It is interesting to note that the United States has also begun to readjust its posture in regard to trade with Communist China. Within the past year, the ban on all material transactions of a commercial or financial nature between the U.S. citizen and a Communist Chinese agency has been modified. This ban had been in effect since December 1951. The first exception was made in July 1969, when the State Department announced that an American citizen traveling abroad could bring home with him up to $100 worth of Chinese merchandise, so long as it was not intended for resale or for commercial use. On December 23, 1969, the ceiling of $100 and a requirement that the goods enter the United States with the traveler were removed. In addition, certain tax-exempt organizations, such as museums, were allowed the same import privileges. More important, the foreign branches and subsidiaries of U.S. firms were allowed to trade with China so long as Chinese goods were not imported into the U.S. Each such change in itself may not be dramatic, but overall they reflect important policy changes.

The forces that can bind Eastern Europe and the NATO countries together are potentially more powerful than those that pull them apart. Government leaders at all levels must exploit every available means to build bridges between East and West. Trade, with its many collateral benefits, is the most effective bridge on which to concentrate our thoughts and energies. ◉

Postscript

After this paper was written the Eastern bloc countries abandoned their long-standing policy of keeping each bilateral trade relationship in balance. This historic shift opened the way to a far more rapid expansion of East-West trade than was deemed possible in 1970. What fueled the expansion, however, was the increase in credit envisaged in this paper.

Western credits have financed a great amount of Eastern European development and have helped bring East and West together. But the very magnitude of those credits has now become something of a problem in itself, as discussed in the following paper.

DUELING AND DEALING WITH THE RUSSIANS

(1977)

An examination of the new problems that have grown out of the rapid expansion of East-West trade: the Soviets, piling up a huge debt to the West, are importing technologically advanced goods that strengthen their war potential....A suggestion that further credits to the East bloc be linked to progress on disarmament, to the reduction of tensions, and to other world concerns.

Imagine—in a variation on an old Three Musketeers plot—two cavaliers in a life-and-death duel. Exhausted, they pause for a moment to catch their breath. "Excuse me," says one, with a flourish of courtesy, "but I'm short of cash just now. Could you lend me forty-five gold pieces? I'll pay you interest, of course."

"Certainly," says his more affluent opponent, tossing over the money. "Business is business—and I know you are a gentleman who honors his debts."

"Thank you," responds the borrower. He promptly flips the bag of coins to an itinerant swordsmith who, in return, hands him a longer, sharper blade for the next phase of the duel.

Business is not always just business. As a businessman, I have dealt in the international arena, and as a frequent U.S. delegate to United Nations conferences, I have dueled there as well. Unhappily, I must report that the wealthier swordsman is us; the borrower is the Soviet bloc whose growing military power is being financed by the United States, Western Europe, and Japan. The blades get longer and sharper; the disarmament talks seem to get nowhere. I think it is time to examine the connection between the expanding mili-

This article appeared in *The Wharton Magazine,* University of Pennsylvania. Winter 1978.

tary strength of the Warsaw Pact countries and their huge expanding external debt. The debt of the member countries of the Council for Mutual Economic Assistance (CMEA), an Eastern bloc trade organization composed of the U.S.S.R., Bulgaria, Czechoslovakia, the German Democratic Republic, Hungary, Poland, and Romania, is the debt of the same countries that make up the Warsaw Pact.

The nations of the Soviet bloc now owe the West about $45 billion. As overall East-West trade accelerates (it tripled between 1970 and 1975) and the Communist nations continue to buy more from the industrialized West than they can sell, the total indebtedness soars ever higher. In 1975, for example, the Communists imported $30.8 billion worth of goods from the West, about $12 billion of it on credit; in 1976, their deficit was $9 billion.

The very structure of East-West trade itself invites Eastern bloc deficits—or at least makes them almost impossible to overcome. Many of the Communist imports are capital goods on long-term orders that cannot be cut back without disrupting development projects already begun. One such project is the $6 billion Orenberg natural gas pipeline running 1700 miles from gas fields in the Urals to connect with an existing pipeline at the Soviet Czechoslovak border. The new line requires massive imports of pipe and equipment, financed by a Eurodollar loan that is scheduled to be paid off with gas piped through the existing line across Czechoslovakia to Austria, West Germany, and Italy.

Other projects of this kind include joint coal and timber developments with the Japanese in Siberia, a pulp mill at Ust'Illimsk, and the production of iron ore and ferro-alloys near Kursk. Polish projects include a $285 million expansion of the Polkowice copper mining complex, and a $250 million tractor plant.

In these joint ventures, future output has been mortgaged to pay for the capital equipment already imported. We can therefore forget the popular notion that Communist countries with planned economies can merely push a button to reduce imports and thereby balance their trade. The Eastern European countries are locked into a trade pattern that demands continued borrowing from the West. The growth and development of East-West trade is vastly more important to the CMEA countries, for it provides them with the means for their industrial modernization and economic expansion, and for their improved military capability as well.

About one third of the borrowed money has come from Western governments, either in the form of direct export credits provided by official agencies or as bank loans guaranteed by a government. Britain, France, West Germany, and Japan, countries that depend heavily on exports, offer these credits almost automatically.

Commercial bank credits at relatively low interest rates account for another $20 billion or so. The rates remain low (under 7½ percent at present) for several reasons: the Communist nations pay up promptly; there is not much loan demand in other parts of the world right now; and the banks compete vigorously to lend in the seemingly lucrative and growing Eastern bloc market. Since the Communist nations, remarkably, find about 80 percent of their commercial credits in the Eurodollar market, it is difficult to figure out just where the money originates.

We do know that not much of it is coming from the United States. We are barred from granting any significant amount of official credit to the Communist countries by a web of legal restrictions, including the Jackson Amendment to the 1974 Trade Act, which links trade to Soviet emigration policies. United States law theoretically also prohibits American banks from lending money to the Soviet Union, Czechoslovakia, or East Germany because those three countries are still technically in default on prewar obligations to the United States. But foreign branches of U.S. banks and agricultural export credits, which can be substantial, are exempt from these laws. At the end of 1976, U.S. commercial bank lending to Communist nations alone totalled $4.3 billion, or about one-fifth of the Eastern bloc's total bank borrowings.

Of course, the increased trade made possible by this river of credit is assumed to be beneficial to everybody. When we examine just what it is that is being traded, however, some worrisome questions arise. Manufactured goods account for about 80 percent of Eastern European imports but only about 30 percent of their exports. Delving further, we find that products carrying a large component of technological value, machinery, equipment, pipe and chemicals, for example, make up about half of all the goods going to the Eastern nations and only about 14 percent of the products coming back. Most of what comes back is raw material such as lumber, fuels, and minerals (about 60 percent) and labor-intensive products, including textiles and processed food (about 25 percent).

The breakdown for the Soviet Union alone is even more lopsided than for the other Communist countries as a whole: Of the U.S.S.R.'s exports to the West, 85 percent consists of raw materials, and only 8 percent technology. But 43 percent of the Soviet Union's purchases in the West is made up of the products of advanced technology. This modern, sophisticated hardware, obtained largely on credit, enables the Soviets to update their industrial plant and sharpen their military sword.

In every year since 1970 the Soviets have spent more money on their military establishment than the United States. The Soviet defense budget actually increased by about 3 percent a year during this period, while the rate of growth of the Soviet economy declined. U.S.S.R. defense spending runs between 11 percent and 14 percent of GNP, compared to 5 percent of GNP for the U.S. The 1975 Soviet budget of $114 billion is 40 percent greater than the comparable U.S. budget in constant dollar terms. Clearly, the Soviet Union and other Communist nations are able to maintain large and growing military forces, while investing in ambitious development programs, only because they can borrow from the West. Every dollar they borrow for trade and development releases an equivalent amount of regular domestic revenue for military use. (Soviet military expenditures also reflect an enormous second front with China.)

Up to now, Western lenders have ignored these political and military realities, and Western political leaders and diplomats have mostly overlooked the leverage that their bankers and the financial departments of their governments could give them. As funds are provided to Communist countries in one European capital, disarmament negotiations are stalled in another, and smoldering international problems trouble every continent.

The world has become too complex and too dangerous for us to allocate capital on financial criteria alone. Credit should be linked to disarmament, to reduction of forces, to overall détente, to peaceful solutions of border tensions, to aid for the developing countries. Perhaps, to give one example, the Communist nations could be dragged into the International Monetary Fund and the World Bank by making some credits conditional on membership. That would go a long way toward alleviating rivalries and competitive tensions in the developing countries.

It will not be easy to change our lending habits. There will always be bankers to succumb to the lure of profit and governments to heed their constituents' clamor for export assistance come what may. But the large governmental role in credit management offers a gleam of opportunity. Even as they grant export credits today, the political leaders of Western Europe and Japan surely know that the world economy will be no better tomorrow unless military confrontations are reduced, unless our capital, our raw materials, our energy sources and our labor are put to more rational and productive use.

An even greater opportunity awaits the United States, which is still hobbled by archaic trade laws. It is time to open our loan window wider, rattle our coins, and make very clear that we will deal—if a deal can halt the armaments madness. That makes much more sense than rattling a saber, or buying a new one. ◉

6
LOOKING AHEAD

THE U.S.-SINO-SOVIET TRIANGLE: A VISION FOR THE FUTURE

(1978)

An explanation of why the future of the world economy depends on cooperation between the United States, Russia, and China, and some suggestions on how to bring it about.

Consider first the Soviet Union, whose authoritarian regime has achieved military parity with the United States but is only on the threshold of the automobile age. It has a grand total of 4.7 million cars, almost exactly the number of automobiles registered in the state of Florida. Consider also that China, the most populous and most controlled society in the world, with vast natural resources, has barely begun to experience the Industrial Revolution. What are we to make of these interplays between ideology and economics? They clearly create problems for the United States—but may offer opportunities as well.

The wars and confrontations that have erupted over the last three decades and that threaten the peace today have come about from attempts by economic, political, and social systems to impose their ideologies on world events. The proponents of communism and democracy—and such political variations as nazism, socialism, and fascism—are often convinced that only their own particular brand of social, economic, and political arrangements can produce worldwide salvation. Too often these messianic powers are willing to go to war to prove the point.

Their hope of imposing their ideology permanently on others defies history. The world has never been entirely dominated by one society, one system, or one

July 1978, written specifically for this volume.

ruler, though many have tried. In the West, the nearest success was probably achieved by the Roman emperors, who did for a time bring under one roof the entire civilized world—as they knew it. But even as the glory of Rome was at its height, the later Han emperors in China and the Gupta kings of India were also dominating the world *they* knew. Almost simultaneously these three distinct, highly developed societies existed, each claiming and believing themselves to be paramount, each barely aware of the others. Later, Islam spread its power and religion through a vast stretch of the world, from Mecca westward across North Africa to Spain and eastward through the Middle East and across the reaches of India and on to the Philippines—but most of China and most of Europe never succumbed.

Strains in the Bloc

Today technology and trade link the power centers of the planet. But language, social customs, and political processes have evolved in diverse ways in different parts of the world. So it remains unlikely that any socioeconomic system will be able to supplant all others and dominate the world. The nations of the world must recognize that other systems have a right to exist—and will exist. Accepting this reality leads to a pragmatic policy of dynamic cooperation rather than confrontation and conflict. The interdependence of the world makes it impossible for the United States to ignore any other region or system as the Romans could ignore China and India.

The three superpowers have compelling economic incentives for a stronger framework of cooperative relationships. Each possesses something of use to the other: the oil and minerals of Siberia, the grain harvests of the American plains, the matchless American apparatus for raising capital, and China's enormous work force, potential markets, and energy resources. Opportunities for development are vast. It is futile for economists to study previous import and export movements between the United States, Russia, and China and then use these statistics to gauge future potentialities. Previous levels of cooperative achievement could be completely dwarfed by the results of dynamic cooperation.

At present, as we learn of the steady improvement in the Soviet Union's military force and have near confrontations with the Soviets, we may wonder whether stability and East-West cooperation is possible or is just wishful thinking. But the Soviet bloc itself is beset by internal divisions. Language and cultural differences among the Warsaw Pact countries make some of them reluctant to support Soviet adventures. Within the Soviet Union proper, the static population of European Russia compared to the population growth of the U.S.S.R.'s Asian areas creates further tensions and strains. Agricultural failures and economic dislocations are also hidden behind the formidable facade of Soviet power. Unsatisfied consumer appetites rise. Dissidents raise their voices. All of these strains, plus, of course, the military strength of the West and the long, uneasy border with China, must have a cautioning effect on the Politburo. There is good reason for the Soviet Union to be in a compromising, opportunistic mood. This could be the time to shift from our policy of détente to an attempt at dynamic cooperation.

Superpower Opportunities

For many years the less-developed world was regarded as the area in which the greatest expansion of trade would take place. The inflation of the past few years—especially the soaring cost of energy—has reduced the potential of many non-oil developing nations. This has contributed to the recessionary tendencies in the West, making it necessary to look elsewhere for additional trade opportunities.

Inflation has been difficult enough for industrial nations to handle. But the developing countries, with their smaller-sized economies and inadequate economic infrastructure, have had to divert a disproportionate part of their borrowing capacity to provide funds for last year's fuel. Their reserves have flowed to the OPEC treasuries. The OPEC group, for its part, has so far failed to work adequately with the West in offering assistance and credit, particularly when one considers how much the rise in oil prices contributed to the problem. Debts of the less-developed countries (L.D.C.'s) have grown rapidly and have reached a level that permits very little, if any, further escalation. Long range, their main economic hope lies in improved growth of the large scale economies of the West and the two Communist superpowers. Trade for the L.D.C.'s expansion must be based on credits, for which this country has the primary power. Credits require an extended period of political stability for repayment, so the future shape of the world economy more likely than ever will be determined by the relationships among the United States, Russia, and China.

It is one of the great ironies of our era that the possibilities of the greatest growth and stability for the democratic world lies in this triangular relationship. The United States has an enormous advantage: it is able to deal with both China and the Soviet Union, while these two superpowers have cut themselves off from each other over ideological and nationalistic differences. The United States could assert its leadership role (the European Common Market and Japan, at least initially, are making the first moves), and if the Soviet Union continues to confront us with hostile actions in Europe, Africa, the strategic Middle East and elsewhere, we could then turn more readily to economic cooperation with China.

154

The East's Need for Credit

The economic development of the Soviet Union and her East European neighbors requires the continued import of vast amounts of machinery and manufactured goods. These imports can only be obtained on credit, for at present the Eastern bloc countries cannot export enough to the West to pay for them. The U.S. government, itself, has vast resources available to finance this trade, supplemented by credits from the private sector powered by our remarkable, successful system of capital accumulation. We have not yet entered this credit market on the scale we could, and our West European allies are far ahead of us.

Part of our failure can be traced to legal restrictions, but an even more important handicap is our traditional attitude toward exports. Favored as we have been, until recently, with an ever expanding domestic market for the output of our farms and factories, we have not viewed the promotion of exports as a vital element of economic policy. Our European allies and Japan, on the other hand, have always depended on exports to pay for necessary raw materials, and they have learned how useful export credits can be. Now that U.S. foreign trade is far out of balance it is clearly time to change our ways.

A Credit Breakthrough

To the Soviets, who have been so intransigent, we should try large-scale, conditional U.S. government and private credits. The condition: they agree to a sharp and dramatic reduction in armaments of all kinds as part of a new framework of cooperation in other areas. An agreement coupling massive new credits with disarmament could be a historic breakthrough. (For a more detailed discussion of the potential benefits of such a credits-for-disarmament arrangement, see "Dueling and Dealing With the Russians," page 142.)

The Soviet bloc is large in scale and includes the countries of Eastern Europe who share a common cultural heritage with the West. As much as we would wish that this political grouping had achieved its economic power through democratic means, we cannot turn the clock back. These countries suggest an opportunity for economic cooperation on a scale that does not exist in countries smaller in size, politically unstable, and which operate with a much more fragile infrastructure and under an entirely different framework of historical customs.

The Chinese Opportunity

China presents perhaps an even better long-range opportunity. Although the Chinese leaders have rejected even their own country's past cultural traditions, as well as our social and economic structure, they are striving to attain a level of development long since reached by the industrialized nations. To consolidate their strength and to respond to their people's desires for an improved standard of living, the Peking leaders are beginning to accommodate to Western technology and trade—without altering their political system. Increasingly they are likely to recognize the massive opportunities for development inherent in Western credits and technology. The United States can and should play a leading role in that process.

One potential field for development is oil. The oil reserves off the China coast are of global significance. They are currently estimated at perhaps triple those of the United States. To locate this oil, to drill it, to refine it, and to distribute it on a major scale will require an enormous input of capital and technology.

It is unrealistic to believe that if the United States refuses to participate in the development of China that the development will not take place. The technology that China needs is also available from Western Europe and Japan. Our industrialized allies in Western Europe, Japan, and elsewhere, have already accorded full diplomatic recognition to the Peoples Republic of China and have shown no reluctance whatever in providing credits and technology.

In February 1978, to cite one example, Japan signed a $20 billion trade pact with China. Under the agreement, which runs for eight years, Japan will ship steel mills, steel, construction materials, and machinery to China in exchange for oil and coal. At about the same time, China signed a five-year trade agreement with the European Economic Community giving both parties most-favored-nation status, with the objective of doubling two-way trade presently aggregating over two billion dollars annually.

Obviously it would be far better for us to join with our allies and develop a coordinated Western approach.

Obstacles to Trade With China

At the present time there are three specific obstacles of varying magnitudes standing in the way of our economic cooperation with China: (1) the Johnson Act of 1934; (2) the Jackson Amendment of 1975 and, most formidable; (3) the Taiwan impasse.

The first two of these obstacles are of our own making and could be done away with readily. The Johnson Act of 1934 prohibits any agency of the U.S. government from lending money to any foreign country against which U.S. citizens have outstanding financial claims. China fits into this category but the amounts involved are modest and this should be a relatively simple matter to resolve.

The so-called Jackson Amendment controls economic relations with any country that prevents its people from freely emigrating. It was aimed at the Soviet Union, which limits Jewish migration to Israel, but it also

157

applies to the rigid emigration controls in China. Under the amendment's terms, the United States cannot grant most-favored-nation tariff rates or extend credits to any country with such controls. If China were to let her people go where they wished the world might be engulfed by a massive wave of migration that could upset the economies and societies of many lands. It makes no sense to isolate China for holding to a policy that we, pragmatically, and by our own immigration restrictions, approve.

The issue of Taiwan is more complex, and it will require hard political decisions in both Washington and Peking to resolve. In the Shanghai Communique of 1972, the United States states that it "does not challenge" the position that "all Chinese on either side of the Taiwan Strait maintain there is but one China and that Taiwan is part of China." Although this statement represented progress of sorts, it was so cautiously and ambiguously worded that it permits the United States to continue to recognize the Nationalist government on Taiwan while simultaneously dealing with the Peoples Republic, but only through a "liaison office" in Peking.

The United States, of all the major nations in the Western Alliance, including Japan, stands alone in not having full diplomatic relations with Peking. Only the Ivory Coast, Jordan, South Korea, Liberia, Saudi Arabia, South Africa, the Vatican, and ten of the smaller Latin American countries join the United States in the diplomatic fiction that full sovereignty recognition cannot be worked out with mainland China. Thus the United States, a nation which claims leadership of half the world, finds itself at the end of a lonely limb.

At the heart of the problem, of course, is the 1955 treaty under which the United States is obligated to defend the Nationalist government on Taiwan if it is attacked. The Peking government, based on the fact that Taiwan had been under Chinese control for about 200 years before the Japanese annexed it in 1895 by force of arms, and that no nation questioned its return to China after World War II, declares with dogged and persistent logic that Taiwan is purely an internal matter. It asserts that normalization of relations with the United States cannot take place until the United States abrogates the 1955 treaty and withdraws all remaining military advisers from the island. The United States is insisting that it will not withdraw without a convincing pledge from the Peoples Republic that it will not try to take Taiwan by force.

Potentially this problem could be stabilized as effectively as the situation between East Germany and West Germany. We may never be able to dismantle this roadblock completely, but neither may we have to, so long as we skillfully prevent it from paralyzing our relationship.

The origin of the U.S. predicament grew out of a number of far-reaching foreign policy miscalculations, but particularly the expectation of a continuing Sino-Soviet alliance. Our continuing military and economic support of the Chiang Kai-shek government on Taiwan was primarily part of a world-wide effort by the United States to contain what we perceived as an aggressive Sino-Soviet alliance. NATO was the line of defense in the West, and Korea, Japan, and Taiwan were to be the containing wall to the East. But then Stalin died. After that, the historic hostility between China and Russia reasserted itself.

Despite the growing estrangement of these two great powers and the change in the character of the Soviet leadership following the death of Stalin, U.S. leaders remained obsessed with the possibility of a Sino-Soviet combination dominating the world. Washington regarded the short-lived period of Sino-Soviet amity as a continuing one even though it no longer existed. This misconception persisted at high levels in Washington and tended to nourish the distorted views that led to the tragedy of Vietnam.

We are now in a different period requiring new perspectives. The key element to unlock the entire puzzle

159

could be a new offer of credits and technology on a vast scale to modernize and develop China's economy. This offer would provide the background and the incentive for stabilizing the Taiwan question and other Far Eastern problems. The Chinese on Taiwan must decide whether and how the social and economic structure that exists on Taiwan will coexist with that on the mainland. For their part, the Peking leaders must be induced to provide some kind of declared assurance that the peace of the region will not be disturbed.

Moreover, the Nationalist's military forces taken together with Taiwan's bustling economy are enough to make costly and forbidding any Communist attempt at a military takeover, especially when one keeps in mind the insecurity of the long land border with the Soviet Union on the West.

With the offer of cooperation in the form of huge credits and great technology before them, the leaders of the Peoples Republic may be willing to guarantee what they may regard as requiring too much of an effort to change, that is, the physical safety of the people on Taiwan. At the very least, there is no reason why Taiwan and the Peoples Republic, two parts of China, cannot exist side by side indefinitely, in peaceful dispute, with the legal question of Taiwan's status left unresolved.

It might be argued that the history of the region certainly shows that disputes are more often settled by force than by negotiation. True enough, but it is naive and unproductive for us to remain frozen in an obsolete posture. Nearly thirty years have gone by since the Peoples Republic took over the mainland and the Nationalists fled to Taiwan. The wheel of history is turning. New generations of leaders have come to power on both sides and the emotions of the revolution have cooled. With relations between Peking and Moscow still strained, this is clearly the moment for the United States to try, at least, to open a new era of dynamic economic negotiations with China.

Once this effort gets under way, both with China and

160

the U.S.S.R., dollars now wasted on armaments could be increasingly applied instead to constructive projects to improve economic and social development. But even these savings will pale into insignificance alongside the positive economic benefits that will flow from a policy which allows goods, material, and technological innovations to move freely among the superpowers. For then we will all be interlocked in dependence on each other, war will become much less an alternative, and the true potential impact of an interdependent world economy can be realized. ◉

This book has been typeset in
11 on 13 point Aster with Aster Bold.
The headings have been set
in several sizes of Korinna Bold;
printed by Offset Lithography on Linweave 70lb.
Natural White text, and bound in Holliston Buckram.
The end papers are Strathmore Artlaid 70lb. Nutmeg.
Designed by Sheldon Cotler Inc.